ANCIENT VISITORS TO THE AMERICAS: THE EVIDENCE

ANCIENT VISITORS TO THE AMERICAS: THE EVIDENCE

ISBN: 978-0-9836350-5-4

Compiled by PAUL T. ANGEL
Edited by JOHN R. TIFFANY

On the Cover: Were Irish Monks the first European visitors to North America? Saint Brendan of Clonfert (c. 484–c. 577) is variously called "the Navigator" and "the Voyager." Brendan is chiefly memorable for his voyage to the Isle of the Blessed, as described in the 9th century manuscript *The Voyage of St Brendan the Navigator.* Some have suggested that he journeyed as far as North America. Several notable archeologists and epigraphers insist that Culdee monks were responsible for the many underground stone chambers found in the American northeast and the ancient inscriptions found carved on rocks there. On the cover is a fanciful antique illustration of St. Brendan performing Easter Mass on the back of a whale during one of his voyages.

AMERICAN FREE PRESS

645 Pennsylvania Avenue SE, #100 • Washington, D.C. 20003
TOLL FREE ORDERING: 1-888-699-NEWS • WEBSITE: WWW.AMERICANFREEPRESS.NET

ANCIENT VISITORS TO THE AMERICAS: THE EVIDENCE

AMERICAN FREE PRESS 2014

TABLE OF CONTENTS

THE ESTABLISHMENT
IS FINALLY CATCHING ON

The recognition of transatlantic contacts has come to be known by the label of "diffusionism." Basically, this Revisionist theory focuses on how the indigenous cultures of America are not original but have borrowed extensively from European visitors to these shores from before the time of Columbus. Interestingly, the old definition of diffusionism was the theory that civilization started in what is now Iraq and eventually worked its way westward, finally enlightening those backward savages called Europeans. This was expressed in Latin as "*ex oriente lux*," or, "the light of civilization comes from the east."

The new theory of diffusionism is that civilization started in Europe and eventually spread around the world, finally enlightening such distant lands as China, the Americas etc. This could be called "*ex europa lux*." Of course, this does not rule out the "Atlantean" theory, of an extremely ancient white culture (which may have spanned much of the globe at one time). It is even possible that Atlantis, if there was such a thing, may have been here in the Americas, and that these continents may be the homeland of *Homo sapiens sapiens*, and/or of the white race (see the book *American Genesis*, by Jeffrey Goodman: Summit Books, New York, 1981). Kennewick Man could be one example showing that Caucasian people (known to all as the "white Americans") were here before the Mongoloid American Indians.

The January 2000 issue of *Atlantic Monthly* featured a cover article called "The Diffusionists Have Landed," by Marc K. Stengel, and running on for nearly 10,000 words. The article is notable because it verifies what Revisionists been saying for years and shows that the establishment media is finally realizing that Christopher Columbus was not the first white visitor to these shores. Scholar Virginia Steen-McIntyre, for instance, has presented evidence supporting the idea that stone-age hominids in Mexico dated back to 250,000 years ago. More recently, information—citing the celebrated Dr. Louis Leakey (now deceased)—has come to light suggesting the hominid presence in California may date back 500,000 years ago. Authors such as Arlington Mallery and Jeffrey Goodman, Ph.D. have been writing amazing tomes about early man in the Americas for decades.

We might also point out that Paul H. Chapman has documented a wealth of information showing that Norse exploration in North America was widespread.

There is also a strong indication that ancient Kelts, Kelt-Iberians and Phoenicians (Carthaginians) made it to America and left their mark in the many underground stone chambers of New England. Spread across America's Northeast are inscriptions in stone carved in ogam and Punic scripts.

Even *The Chicago Tribune* jumped on the diffusionist bandwagon, with an April 6, 2000 article by Michael Kilian, in which he reports on recent findings of the Society for American Archeology. One of the traditionally "old" archeological sites in the New World is near Clovis, New Mexico, where some very finely crafted

A 6th century A.D. Mayan wooden figure with a handlebar mustache—something most American Indians find impossible to grow.

spearheads were found in 1935, known as Clovis points. At one time, these were the oldest known artifacts that proved human habitation in America, and they have been dated to 13,000 years ago. All evidence of humans in America from that era is now known as "Clovis." It was assumed, without any real evidence, by the court historians that the Clovis people were Mongoloids who came via the Bering land bridge around 13,500 years ago, although they really did not want to give man credit for arriving in America so early, as the orthodox estimate had been that the first settlers arrived to these shores only 11,000-12,000 years ago.

Of late, a number of extremely ancient pre-Clovis sites have been popping up, many of them in what is now the Southeastern United States. These are so ancient that there is no way the court historians can "bend the rules" to include them into their dogma. One such site was found in Pennsylvania, another in the Carolinas and another in Florida. However, the site reported on by Mr. Kilian is at Cactus Hill, Virginia, south of Richmond. Officially the dig is known as the "Nottoway River Survey." Dennis Stanford, chairman of the anthropology department at the Smithsonian Institution, is on the team. Stanford created quite a firestorm with his 2013 book *Across Atlantic Ice*, in which he presents his evidence that the Solutrean culture is the only possible culture that could have introduced this advanced projectile point technology. Nowhere in Asia can we find this type of bifacially carved stone weaponry.

Stanford says he has spent a career tramping around Asia and the arctic and the high plains and never found any antecedents there for Clovis. Nor has anybody else. In a 1991 paper, he suggested that Clovis developed out of an existing population in the Southeast. The Cactus Hill material seems to fill that bill. Artifacts that include tools have been found at Cactus Hill, says *The Tribune*, and have been dated to about 20,000 years before the present! (The "Mongoloids First" theorists have no answer for this, as they insist that the Asians could not have crossed the Bering Land Bridge until approximately 9,000 B.C. because it did not even exist before that.)

To reiterate: The Cactus Hill artifacts resemble those used by Europeans of about 22,000 years ago in the Solutrean culture of northern Spain. Cactus Hill may prove to be a giant step in advancing North American archeology and anthropology. But the "politically correct" crowd does not like it.

Then there is the Kensington Rune Stone. This artifact is clearly genuine evidence of the presence of Vikings and Goths—and perhaps even Templars—in what is today the central United States in medieval times. Yet still most establishment works matter-of-factly dismiss its authenticity, and the barely literate farmer who discovered it on his property was hounded to his grave by the deniers. Two of his children killed themselves from the constant slander.

The scholars and researchers working for THE BARNES REVIEW

history magazine,* based in Washington, D.C., from the inception of the magazine in 1994, have published the fact that good, hard evidence points to a vast array of Old World visitors to America hundreds and thousands of years before Columbus. Old Norse sagas even tell of their discovering prior colonies of what were apparently Kelts living on the eastern seaboard. English explorers later encountered natives who had blond hair and blue eyes.

All of this is contrary to the dogma of the court historians, who maintain that the first people to come to these shores were of the Mongoloid race and the first Europeans here were Vikings. The establishment further maintains that the cultures of America, such as the Maya and the Incas, developed in total isolation from the Old World. Supposedly only "cranks" and "kooks" would consider the possibility that Europeans came here before Columbus, say academics who uphold anthropological orthodoxy at universities and research institutes. Now the establishment isolationists are finally being forced to recognize the ever-increasing mound of evidence for diffusionism.

We don't mind saying we told you so. ❖

—Paul T. Angel
Managing Editor
The Barnes Review

*All of the material in this book was gleaned from issues of The Barnes Review (TBR), especially the September/October 2001 issue, which is now, unfortunately, out of print. For more about TBR, visit www.BarnesReview.com.—Ed.

He is painted here in a mixture of Indian and American garb, but dress him up in German clothes and full-blooded Mohawk Joseph Brant, aka Thayendanegea (1742-1807), would look at home on any street of Frankfurt or Munich, Germany. The celebrated chief was for some time a missionary among the Mohawk, translating the Book of Common Prayer and part of the New Testament into his Indian language. A Freemason, he aided the British in both the French and Indian War and the wars against American Indian leader Pontiac. Throughout the American Revolution he fought against the Americans, leading many Indian raids, although the Iroquois Confederacy, to which the Mohawk tribe belonged, was professedly neutral.

REDISCOVERING THE FORGOTTEN WHITE ANCESTORS OF MANY AMERICAN INDIANS

BY J.S. SLAYMAKER

Voluminous works in circulation today, although politically incorrect, set forth historically sound theories regarding the origins of the early Americans. As professional opinion is somewhat divided among historians, anthropologists and archeologists, controversy seems to be the ultimate rule of the day, both within and without the academic community.[1] The question here seems to be exactly where the first migrants came from and what other Old World voyagers joined them before the time of Christopher Columbus. Although this brief article is by no means exhaustive, and because such information is open to various interpretations, there is simply not enough evidence to satisfy everyone completely.[2]

Hubert Bancroft, for example, concedes that neither is there supportive evidence nor a possibility of stray ships of various nations and sporadic times and places which may have landed upon American coasts, nor will he concede to voyages specifically designed for such a purpose before Norsemen of the 10th century A.D. Yet he will contradictorily admit that it was extremely probable that there was some form of communication taking place by sailing vessel as the only means of travel across oceans and therefore the only means of intercontinental communication until well into the 19th century.[3]

The theory that Christopher Columbus was the first white man to set foot in the Americas should be immediately dispelled. Of course, everyone agrees that the Vikings were here earlier, although the extent of Viking contact with America continues to be hotly debated. But we also have records of Sumerians, Dravidians and Phoenicians going to sea in large, sturdy and well-rigged ships, far more advanced than those being constructed in the late 15th century A.D. by Europeans. Some of these records go as far back as 2100 B.C. Ancient tablets from Sumer tell of their monarchs sailing to the "Land Beyond the Western Sea," where Sumerian monuments and colonies were established.[4] Yet scholars today are unsure on whether this could be a reference to ancient America.

One surety among scholars, though, is that considerable progress in the area of navigation was achieved in the ancient world. Contrary to popular belief, the idea that the Earth is spherical in shape was in no way original with Galileo Galilei, but was known from a much earlier period.

Harvard Professor Barry Fell recounts an incident as told by Diodorus Siculus of Carthaginian settlements established in what now appears to be either South America or Cuba. According to Diodorus, Phoenician ships were blown far off course beyond the Pillars of Hercules (now known as the Strait of Gibraltar) and into the Atlantic Ocean. After several days of sailing to the west

EVIDENCE OF A MINOAN PRESENCE IN THE ANCIENT AMERICAS?

Now deceased epigrapher Barry Fell and others believe the great seafarers of the Minoan culture also made it to America well before the Vikings. They point to stones like the one here, which displays a script that closely resembles Minoan writing dating back to 2000–1000 B.C.

of Africa, they came upon an enormous island, which was not only fertile but watered by navigable rivers. Before long, the discovery was well known to both those of not only Carthage but also to the Tyrrhenians of Italy. Carthaginian settlements were founded here but were soon disbanded and prohibited from any further encroachment due to the official policies of Carthage.[5]

Some Chilean Indians have a tradition that claims their ancestors came from the west. Chippewa Indians of North America claim their ancestors traveled from a distant land in which "bad" people lived, that these ancestors had crossed a "lake," filled with islands, where the ice and snow exist continually. Algonquins teach similarly of a foreign origin and distant sea voyage. The tradition preserved by the Olmecs was that they had been eastern peoples. The Yucatees traditionally believe that they too were originally eastern people, having come only after passing through a sea which God made dry for them.[6]

French Commandant Jules Cauvet published a thesis from Algiers in 1930 with the idea of certain groups of Berbers having the same ethnic names as certain Indian tribes in America. Nowhere else in the world are such American names found outside of the Berber tribes themselves. Ethnic names have at various times throughout the past been discovered by archeologists in their following of a migrating people.

These names are often the final linguistic element to be abandoned after the people's language has either been forgotten or absorbed. More than one anthropologist has made the discovery of peoples inhabiting the Sahara Desert possessing similar traits to those of the American Indian. These similarities do not only include names and naming methods, but also include tribal groups who are designated by similar titles, only differing occasionally in prefix or suffix.[7]

Professor Fell notes that America has a long history of discovering—or rather rediscovering—ancient coins and other arti-

This is an old portrait of a Chippewa chief, whose name is unknown. Were it not for his silver nose-ring and other exotic accouterments, he could be mistaken for a native of the British Isles. This is from the Royal Ontario Museum. The Chippewas or Ojibwas still live in fragments of the ancient homeland in Wisconsin and Minnesota, where once they held lakes Superior and Michigan at their disposal. They did very little farming but are said to have fished on a tremendous scale.

facts, but nearly as long is America's history of ignoring such finds. In the early days of the republic, our Founding Fathers and earlier men of learning such as Increase and Cotton Mather, both men of the clergy and founding presidents of Harvard University, studied the Latin language and Roman history; both being required subjects in order to earn any college degree. It was commonly understood among these men that such mementos were left as Roman ships sailed the Atlantic Ocean. After the evolution of the Columbus mystique in American textbooks (and the teaching of our children that until the year 1492 the world was considered to be flat), these discoveries were dismissed and further discoveries were ignored.[8]

It was not until after 1860 that the theory arose that American Indians were descended from Asiatics who migrated across the Bering land bridge. It has been as recent as 1940 that Norsemen were considered by establishment historians as never having ventured to America, and no European was thought to have visited America prior to Columbus.[9]

Needless to say, Professor Fell was not short on his own supply of critics. He has been accused of everything from unsupported speculation to a faulty knowledge of the Algonquian language, leading him to erroneous conclusions, not to mention defective analysis and interpretation. In some cases, he has even been accused of outright fraud, using inscriptions that have been proven to be fakes. Others say that his ideas are no more than well-worn but disproven themes which no respectable archeologist would take seriously.[10] Yet in spite of such criticisms, Professor Fell invalidated these accusations against him, as reliable scholars in some well-respected universities and museums have confirmed the validity of Fell's conclusions.[11]

In fact, there have been some indisputable occurrences which have taken place in various parts of what we now call the United States as it was being settled. The Welsh clergyman Morgan Jones was traveling home to Roanoke, Virginia from South Carolina in 1660 when he fell captive to the Tuscarora Indians. He spent several months among these "white Indians" as they were known in the colonial era, preaching the Gospel to them. He personally believed that his life was spared because of his ability to speak Welsh, a language many of the Tuscarora Indians understood. Rev. Jones concluded that, due to the fairness of their skin, color of their eyes, the circular manner in which they constructed their living quarters and the Druidical order of their religious life, they were of pre-Christian Welsh origin.[12]

In 1801 a certain Lt. Roberts recounted the story of having met with an Indian chief in Washington, D.C. who spoke the Welsh language as fluently as that of any native of Wales. The lieutenant was informed of this being the ancient language of the "Asguaws," a people living some 800 miles northwest of Philadelphia. The In-

THE RACIAL CHARACTERISTICS OF INDIAN TRIBES RUN THE GAMUT

American Indians are not a race of man but cover a vast gamut of racial types from very nearly Caucasoid, through what we think of as typical Plains Indian types, to Mongoloid types who could pass unnoticed in south China, and with occasional ventures into the Negroidal realm. A handsome man, Osceola (1804-38), the famous chief of the Seminoles, a tribe that split off from the Creek Indians, could probably pass for a Lebanese Arab. He led his tribe in their final war against the Anglo-Americans and put up one of the stiffest resistances Indians ever made. This rather imaginative painting (top of page) is titled "Osceola's Method of Signing a Treaty" and depicts a dramatic incident in the great chief's refusal to make peace or cede any part of his tribe's land. The U.S. government responded by trying to exterminate the free Seminoles (Second Seminole War, 1835-42), but failed, although Osceola was perfidiously captured while under a flag of truce in 1838. The war cost thousands of lives and millions of dollars. To this day in Florida there are bands of Seminoles who claim, truthfully, that they have never surrendered to the United States. The Seminole language belongs to the Muskhogean language family. The inset at right shows Osceola in more detail.

dian was himself unfamiliar with the land of Wales but said that it was traditionally believed among his people that their ancestors had come from a distant land that was far to the east, across the great waters. Stationed at a trading post in Illinois, a certain Capt. Davies had written that he had found it to be of a great surprise to find that several of the Welshmen belonging to his company could readily converse with the Indians in Welsh. The Scottish Lord Monboddo, in the 17th century, wrote that many of the Indian tribes throughout Florida spoke a Keltic tongue.[13]

In May of 1773 Thomas Bullitt met with Shawnee Chief Blackfish on behalf of Virginia's "great white father," Lord Dunmore, in hopes that a treaty of peace might be negotiated over settlements that ran just south of the Ohio River, known as Can-Tuckee. Chief Blackfish stated that he neither had the power to negotiate over this land nor the power to grant permission to settle it, for it did not belong to the Shawnees but the ghosts of the murdered "Azgens," a white people from the Eastern Sea. He claimed that the forefathers of the Shawnees had long ago killed off the Azgens but were now in fear of their spirits.[14]

Some historians believe the Azgens mentioned by Blackfish may have been remnants of Sir Walter Raleigh's lost colony at Roanoke, which disappeared without a trace in 1587-1590.

Copper works in the Michigan area have proven to be one of the greatest puzzles in mining technology history. Approximately 5,000 ancient copper mine workings revealed on Lake Superior's northern shore and on nearby Isle Royale date back to 4000 B.C. according to Nigel Davies, although this writer believes his date to be at least 2,000 years premature.[15] According to radiocarbon testing (admittedly one of the more unreliable methods of dating), these operations took place between 2000 and 1000 B.C., which corresponds more closely to the bronze age in Northern Europe. Estimates are that 250,000 tons of copper were removed, although the exact location of where that copper was moved to remains a mystery. Because only a relatively small number of artifacts have been discovered in North America, it is believed that the vast majority of it was transported to Europe.[16]

Coins with Hittite glyphs have been found near Kanab, Utah.[17] However, the most interesting artifact discovered, this writer believes, was in 1827 by a farmer in Brazil. While in his fields he came upon a flat stone with the Greek engraving: "During the dominion of Alexander, the son of Philip, king of Macedon, in the 63rd Olympiad, Ptolemaios." Below the stone were found two swords, a shield and a helmet. The handle of one of the swords bore a portrait of Alexander III; the helmet contained a design which represented the corpse of Hector as he was being dragged around the walls of Troy by Achilles.[18]   ❖

ENDNOTES:

1 Davies, Nigel, *Voyagers to the New World*, New York, William Morrow & Co., 1979, 7.

2 *Ibid.*, 16-19.

3 Bancroft, Hubert H., *The Works of Hubert Howe Bancroft*; Vol. 5, "The Native Races of the Pacific States," San Francisco, A.L. Bancroft & Co., 1883, 5: 130,134.

4 Verill, A. Hyatt, and Verill, Ruth, *America's Ancient Civilizations*, New York, G.P. Putnam's Sons, 1953, 105.

5 Fell, Dr. Barry, *Saga America*, New York, The New York Times Book Club, Times Books, 1983, 72-73.

6 Bancroft, Hubert H., *op. cit.*, 5: 22.

7 Van Sertima, Ivan, *They Came Before Columbus*, New York, Random House, 1976, 252-54.

8 Fell, *Saga America*, op. cit., 27.

9 *Ibid.*, 15.

10 Davies, *op. cit.*, 153-56.

11 *Saga America*, op. cit., 24.

12 Spencer, Morton W., *The Missing Links; or The Anglo-Saxons, The Ten Tribes of Israel*, Hollis, New York, the Holliswood Press, 1901, 14.

13 Bancroft, *op. cit.*, 5: 118-120, 122.

14 Eckert, Allan W., *The Frontiersman*, Boston, Little & Brown, 1967, 70-74.

15 Davies, *op. cit.*, 73.

16 Fell, Dr. Barry, *Bronze Age America*, New Boston, Little & Brown, 1982, 261.

17 Verill, *op. cit.*, 94.

18 Bancroft, *op. cit.*, 5: 123.

J.S. Slaymaker is a Revisionist historian who has been active for many years in publicizing the mysteries of ancient America.

Researcher Trondur Patursson practices his harpoon tossing skill from the bow of a boat made in the old Irish tradition: skins strecthed over a wooden frame and sealed with natural animal oils. It was on a boat like this St. Brendan was alleged to have crossed the Atlantic Ocean.

DID IRISHMEN DISCOVER AMERICA?

BY JOHN TIFFANY

St. Brendan (or Brandan), one of the most famous of Irish saints, was also an abbot. He was born probably about A.D. 489 near the lakes of Killarney in County Kerry, in the area around Tralee. He founded many important Irish monasteries throughout the country. For five years he was in the charge of the famous virginal St. Ita of Killeedy (also spelt Ite or Oda), of whom many stories are told. In perhaps A.D. 559, Brendan founded the monastery of Clonfert. But that was only a part of his works. He was quite a traveler, always moving about by sea; and even the court historians will go so far as to admit that he went to Scotland and perhaps Wales.

According to various medieval legends, Brendan, by then in his 70s, and a band of monks embarked on a seven-year voyage through the Atlantic in search of the "Promised Land," where, it seems, another Irish monk, known as St. Finbarr, had been before. (Unfortunately, not much is known about this particular St. Finbarr; there are five Irish saints of this name.) The legends, which were known in most of the European languages in the middle ages, recount Brendan's amazing adventures. The saint is said to have eventually discovered a mysterious land (possibly the American mainland), through which flowed a great river. Many people, especially the "court historians," have tended to dismiss the Brendan legends as merely fantastic myths—the product of overheated medieval imaginations.

The saint is said to have visited a country far across the Atlantic Ocean, which Irish popular tradition identifies as America, and certain passages in the story suggest that St. Brendan may have reached Bermuda and the Bahamas.

Here is a summary of the Brendan legend, with modern interpretation identifying the places visited and some of the phenomena the monks observed:

1. St. Brendan and his companions, heading northward from Ireland, come to a rocky isle with no obvious landing place. After sailing around it, they discover a single cove, where they go ashore (St. Kilda).

2. They sail onward to an island in northern seas where there are many sheep and a monastic community (the Faeroes).

3. They wander back and forth in an archipelago, staying ashore for long periods (the Shetlands).

4. They sail north to another island, a place of fire and smoke, where it looks as if a great number of smiths are at work on glowing metal. As they watch, the mass blazes and becomes molten (to Iceland, witnessing an eruption of the volcano Hekla).

·5. After returning to a point previously visited and obtaining advice, they sail west for 40 days.

6. They are surrounded by darkness, which is said to be the prelude to arrival in the land they are seeking (fog on the Newfoundland banks).

7. They come to a huge crystal pillar in the sea. (They sight an iceberg drifting south with the Greenland current.)

8. They reach an inhospitable coast where there are creatures

with tusks and speckled bellies. (They put in briefly at Newfoundland and encounter walruses.)

9. They sail into a semitropical lagoon. (They make for a warmer zone and eventually enter the Bahamas.)

10. They put in at an island and are attacked by small, dark savages (possibly Carib Indians).

11. They sail over transparent waters where they can see a long way down. (Exploring the Caribbean fringes, they notice the famous transparent sea, beloved by modern scuba divers.)

12. They disembark in the Promised Land, which is sunshiny and warm and abounds in fruit. After 40 days of exploration they reach a river. The land seems to stretch indefinitely beyond, and they give up the attempt to find its limit (Florida or the Gulf Coast).

St. Brendan died in c. 577-583 at Enach Duin, Ireland.

In 1976, Tim Severin, a British navigational scholar and adventurer, embarked from Brandon Creek on the Dingle peninsula of County Kerry, in a curragh (coracle) he constructed using the details described by Brendan. His goal was to determine if the legendary voyage of Brendan and his fellow monks was physically possible. They tanned ox hides in a special process, using oak bark, stretched them across a wooden frame of ash (from the tougher, north-facing sides of the trees), sewed them with leather thread and smeared the hides with wool fat, which would impart water resistance. All was in strict accordance with the medieval practices, as nearly as those could be reconstructed by surviving craftsmen. After a remarkable 50-day journey, the reenactors' two-masted ship, christened the *Brendan*, made landfall at Peckford Island, Newfoundland, some 150 miles northwest of the town of St. Johns.

It would not be surprising if Irishmen discovered America prior to the Columbus voyage and even before Leif Eriksson, since they are known to have gotten to the Faeroe Islands and other North Atlantic lands before the Vikings. Indeed, the Viking sagas tell of white men called *Papar*, their word for Christian men, living in Iceland before the Northmen settled on that island. While there is no archeological evidence as yet to prove the presence in Iceland of ancient Irish hermits, *The Book of Icelanders* is considered a very reliable historical source.

A later wave of Irish immigration to America seems to have taken place around A.D. 770, when polytheistic Vikings began to settle in Iceland, pushing the Christian Irish out of that place. They fled the violence-prone pagans and went to Cape Breton Island. This colony was called "*Irland ed Mikla*"—"Greater Ireland"—or "*Huitramannaland*" (literally "white man land")—also called later "Albania" ("the white country"). (Scotland was also called Albania in former times, a corruption of *Alba*, its Gaelic name. The modern republic of Albania, on the other hand, is so called because a medieval Roman visitor compared its scenery to that of the Alban Hills of Italy.)

Their language and religious rites still survived in 1020, but eventually the Micmac Indian tribe assimilated the remnant of the colony.

St. Finbarr may have had access to even earlier Irish records of transatlantic travel: There is ample evidence that America was well known to pre-Christian Kelts, going back to about 800 B.C. (TBR Oct. 1997, Nov. 1997). In this connection, the old Irish name for a land in the west is "*Hy Brasil*," which means "Island of Iron." (The word for iron is "*brzl*" in Ugaritic; the cognate word in Akkadian is "*parzillu*.") Whether or not the so-called Island of *Brasil* visited by pre-Columbian European voyagers was in the country now known as Brazil is unknown, but it is worthy of note that Brazil's chief resource is iron and that 25 percent of the world's known iron ore reserves are in the Brazilian province of Minas Gerais.

Coracles are traditional Keltic watercraft used even to this day by the Welsh people as well as by some in Ireland. It is interesting to note that the Mandan Indians, thought by some scholars to be partly descended from pre-Columbian Welsh voyagers to America, were observed by pioneers to be using primitive, round "bull boats" of wicker covered with hides, very similar to Welsh and Irish coracles. ❖

BIBLIOGRAPHY:

Boutet, Michel-Gerald, *The Celtic Connection*, Stonehenge Viewpoint, Santa Barbara, California, 1996.

Cyr, Donald L., *Megalithic Adventures*, Stonehenge Viewpoint, Santa Barbara, California, 1992.

Cyr, Donald L., ed., *The Diffusion Issue*, Stonehenge Viewpoint, Santa Barbara, California, 1991.

Goodwin, William B., *The Ruins of Great Ireland in New England*, Meador Publishing Co., Boston, 1946.

Gordon, Cyrus, *Before Columbus: Links Between the Old World and Ancient America*, Crown Publishers, New York, 1971.

Severin, Tim, *The Brendan Voyage*, McGraw-Hill Book Co., New York, 1978.

Thompson, Gunnar, *American Discovery*, Argonauts Misty Isles Press, Seattle, 1994.

WEBSITES:

www.castletown.com/brendan.

www.heritage.nf.ca/exploration/brendan.

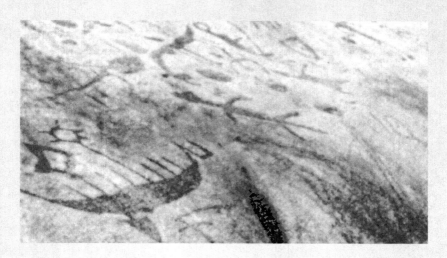

ANCIENT COPPER MINERS LEAVE EVIDENCE?

Above is a petroglyph dating from the bronze age in the Peterborough Petroglyph Park, Ontario. Two ships can be made out, perhaps exploring for copper. Vermont, it seems, was among the earlier New World sites mined for copper (the Elizabeth copper mine at Thetford would be an example), but the workings there were abandoned when the prospectors discovered the abundant copper of Michigan.

ANCIENT MINES & ASTRONOMICAL CHAMBERS

Photographer and investigator Warren Dexter claims that many of Vermont and Michigan's ancient copper mines are associated with underground chambers that are aligned to celestial points. Many of these chambers allow the Sun to penetrate through openings only during the solstices and equinoxes. Many times ancient Keltiberian and Keltic inscriptions are also found in the vicinity. Here is pictured an ancient surface copper mine in Michigan's Upper Peninsula.

SOURCE: *AMERICA'S ANCIENT STONE RELICS* BY WARREN DEXTER

EVIDENCE FOR A LOST WHITE CIVILIZATION IN ANCIENT AMERICA

BY FRANK JOSEPH

O ne of history's greatest mysteries is also one of its least well known: More than 3,000 years ago, at least half a million tons from the world's highest-grade copper ore deposits vanished without a trace from the upper Great Lakes region of North America. But this total (the weight equivalent of 10 Missouri-class battleships) is the minimum, conservative estimate of copper removed in the ancient past. Authorities specializing in Michigan's oldest enigma, such as Fred Rydholm, who lectured on this subject at The Barnes Review's Second International Conference (June 15-17, 2001) and Frank Joseph, point out that the latest research suggests a more realistic figure would be four to six times that amount.[1]

When the first modern Europeans entered the Michigan area during the late 1770s, they stumbled upon the remains of a gargantuan mining operation. More than 5,000 long-abandoned pit mines spread across Keweenaw Peninsula and Isle Royale. On

Michigan's northern shore, the diggings extended for 150 miles, varying in width from four to seven miles through the Trapp Range, which includes three modern counties (Houghton, Ontonagon and Keweenaw). At Isle Royale, the mining area was 40 miles long and averaged five miles across. The pits ran in practically a contiguous line for 30 miles through the Rockland region. If all of the prehistoric Michigan mines were placed end to end, single file, they would form a man-made trench more than five miles long, 20 feet wide and 30 feet deep.

As proof of a former technology far beyond anything known to the resident Indians, some of the pit mines had been excavated more than 60 feet straight down through solid rock. Michigan historian William P.F. Ferguson described the ancient mining enterprise as one "of a colossal nature. It amounted to the turning over of the whole formation to its depth and moving many cubic miles of rock."[2] An average of 1,000 to 1,200 tons of ore was excavated from each pit, yielding about 100,000 pounds of copper per pit.

To achieve such prodigious yields, the prehistoric miners employed techniques that enabled them to work with speed and efficiency. They created intense fires atop a copper-bearing vein, heated the rock to extremely high temperatures, then doused it with water. The rock fractured, and stone tools were used to extract the copper. Deep in the pits, a vinegar mixture was employed to speed spalling (breaking of the rock in layers) and reduce smoke. But how such high temperatures were achieved is part of the enigma. Even especially hot cane fires would take a long time to sufficiently heat the vein for spalling, if at all, because the bottom of a fire is its coolest part. How the ancient miners directed concentrated, acetylene-torch temperatures to the ground is a disturbing question modern archeologists must ponder.

The genius of America's third millennium B.C. miners extended to their equally unknown but astonishingly accurate method for locating copper veins. Every historic Lake Superior mine opened over the last 200 years had been previously worked by the ancients; they mined all the productive veins throughout the whole region. Octave DuTemple, the foremost authority on early Michigan, wrote:

> **As some of these veins did not outcrop at the surface, but were discovered only upon excavation, it is seen that these prehistoric peoples possessed a gift or ability which present-day man would find very valuable.**[3]

Mineralogist Jacob Houghton argued that all the veins had been recently exposed by glacial action, and were therefore easily discernible to the ancient prospectors, who required no extraordinary gift or ability to find the copper. H.H. Winchell, a late 19th-century local historian, likewise believed they simply followed along an observable copper-bearing belt of rock laid bare by freshly retreating glaciers.[4] Houghton nonetheless admitted that:

> **The ancient miners made few mistakes in the selection of deposits to be wrought. In almost every instance in the places where they had carried on extensive mine work, they have been wrought in successful mines of these latter days.**[5]

But more recent understanding about Upper Peninsula geology confirms that the whole region, as it appears today, was virtually unchanged for 5,000 years before the first mines were opened, so the glacier did not expose the copper veins for the prehistoric prospectors, after all.

By way of comparison with their almost forgotten achievement, the first modern mine at Isle Royale was inaugurated in

1771 by British engineers, who failed to extract enough minerals to make their enterprise worthwhile before it had to be shut down. It was not until 70 years later that Michigan's copper sources, all of them known and worked by the ancients 5,000 years before, were found. Their original mines only came to light in 1847. The Calumet and Hecla Conglomerate, employing modern technology and electric power, removed 509 million tons of copper between 1929 and 1949, compared with the minimum estimate of tonnage mined by an unknown people during the heyday of the Egyptian pharaohs.

As mineralogist Roy W. Drier remarked:

> **There is not a mine operating today in the district that has not had its prehistoric workings. The fact was so well established in the early days (of modern mining) that the evidence of ancient work was sought as a guide to present lodes. The development of the Calumet was certainly hastened by the finding of the old mine, and many of the other modern mines owe votes of thanks to these mysterious, unknown, prehistoric workers.**[6]

Nor did they dig up only small fragments. Masses of copper rock weighing 6,000 pounds and more were excavated and raised on well-made crib-work, stone and timber platforms used to lift ponderous materials to the surface. These cribs were usually made of trimmed tree trunks to resemble a log cabin that could be raised by a series of levers and wedges. An example of the massive portions mined in ancient Michigan was the so-called "Ontonagon Boulder." Removed to the Smithsonian Institution in Washington, D.C. around the turn of the 19th century, it weighs no less than five tons. A six-ton copper mass was discovered *in situ* on one of the raised cribs, where it appears to have been abandoned on the day the miners suddenly quit the pits. Partially trimmed of its spurs and projecting points, it was still 10 feet long, three feet wide and two feet thick.

Literally millions of tools used by the ancient miners have been found. Their numbers indicate that a great many men were engaged in extracting huge quantities of copper from upper Michigan over a very long period of time—suggesting that a 500,000-ton estimate of their labors does indeed fall far short of their actual achievement. For example, as far back as 1840, 10 wagon-loads of their stone hammers were taken from a single location near Rockland. Those removed from McCargo Cove, on the north side of Isle Royale, amounted to 1,000 tons. All the mauls were mass-produced in various sizes and types to serve different tasks. Some were only 2.4-pound hand-held tools for finishing and shaping. Others weighed 40 pounds and more. Fastened to cables suspended from a crossbar, they were swung like pendulums to batter the rock face and crush chunks of ore. But most hammers were five to ten pounds, grooved to fit a wooden handle tied around the middle. Generally egg-shaped, they were made from diabase, a hard, tough, fine-grained, igneous rock found in profusion throughout the upper Great Lakes region.

For all their mass production, these ancient hammers were not crudely manufactured. As Drier wrote of his experience:

In examining the tools that have been recovered, one is involuntarily amazed at the perfection of the workmanship and at their identity of form with the tools made for like purposes and used at the present day, the prototypes of the implements of our present civilization. The sockets of the spears, chisels, arrowheads, knives and fleshers are, in nearly all instances, formed as symmetrically and perfectly as could be done by the best smith of the present day, with all the improved aids of his art.[7]

In addition to the superabundant mauls, many other kinds of well-crafted tools were found in the ancient mines. There were finely crafted wooden shovels, copper gads (wedges) and chisels. The mines themselves were not simple pits, but outfitted with surprisingly modern drainage systems to flush out debris and fill via huge trenches, some as long as 500 feet. Well-made wooden buckets and bailers of various sizes were common discoveries.

Basing their conclusions on a conservative estimate of 500,000 tons removed from prehistoric Michigan, researchers believe approximately 10,000 men worked the mines to extract that amount. The freighting of ancient Michigan copper proceeded on a similarly huge scale. Writing in *Ancient American* magazine, John H. Rudolf pointed out that:

> [D]ividing 500,000 tons by 2,000 years gives 250 tons per year, average. Presuming 120 days from June through September to allow open water suitable for travel, 250 tons per year [divided] by 120 days times 2,000 pounds per ton equals 4,166 pounds moved per day. Since copper weighs 556 pounds per cubic foot, it would occupy only 1.8 cubic feet of space per boat. [1.8 x 556 = 1000.8 pounds per boat; this would imply 4166/1000 = 4.2 boats per day.—Ed.] Twenty stacks of copper ingots of 50 pounds apiece would make handling and portaging a laborious but manageable cargo. If the copper was taken out in one grand mass-sailing at the end of the mining season, perhaps by the miners themselves, there would have had to have been a fleet of 120 to 480 ships [or 4.2 x 120 = 504 ships—Ed.], accommodating around 1,920 men.[8]

The time parameters for this vast organizational endeavor are clear. Carbon-dating tests conducted by the University of Michigan in the 1970s demonstrated the mines were worked from around 3000 B.C. to 1200 B.C, peaking in the 13th century B.C.[9] These results were consistent with previous and subsequent C-14 analysis and stratigraphic testing of the pit mines themselves by different institutions, academic and commercial. Interestingly, Michigan copper mining ended as abruptly as it began.

Previous to the close of the fourth millennium, the region had been thinly populated by what archeologists refer to as "paleo-Indians," scattered bands of materially unsophisticated hunter-gatherers to whom farming, pottery and the bow and arrow were unknown. They did pick up "float copper," small chunks deposited on the surface of the ground by retreating glaciers, then battered (annealed) the pieces into decorative, shiny trinkets or the occasional spearhead.

Yet, 5,000 years ago, a labor-intensive undertaking burst into being, as though newly imported and set up by masses of outsiders who already possessed the necessary know-how to install a mining complex. Less than 2,000 years later, it terminated just as suddenly. DuTemple wondered, "Why did these miners leave their operations and implements as though planning on taking up their labors the next day, and yet mysteriously never returned?"[10] Indeed, all Michigan operations were decisively terminated, to all visible signs, in a single day. Tools, mauls, picks, hammers, shovels, crib-work and sleds were all left in place.

These artifacts were first scientifically examined by Wisconsin's leading archeologist, S.A. Barrett, in the early 1930s. "We are not disposed to attribute this work (the ancient copper mines) to the aboriginal inhabitants," he observed. "The keepers, levers, wooden bowls etc are rather indicative of Caucasian ingenuity and art."[11] Dr. James Fisher, professor of mineralogy at the University of Michigan, made a lifetime study of the prehistoric copper miners, concluding, "[T]he civilization of this people was of a much higher order than that of the succeeding races generally referred to as the North American Indians."[12]

Mere consideration of the vessels necessary to transport hundreds of thousands of tons of copper from Isle Royale across Lake Superior's storm-tossed waters did, after all, require something more substantial than birch-bark canoes. Such freighting necessitated deep-hulled sailing ships, which were beyond anything the aboriginals ever envisioned. Another researcher, Jack Parker, asked, "Why is there no link between the ancient miners and the present Indians?"[13] Indeed, Houghton pointed out that their preserved skulls are orthocephalic, occupying "a position between the Indian cranium, which is brachycephalic, and the Teutonic, which is dolichocephalic."[14]

Among the first recent Old World visitors who traveled through the copper mining region in the mid-18th century was the famous French missionary Father Claude Allouez, who saw there a one-foot-tall statue sculpted entirely from a single copper nugget to represent a man "with a beard like a European."[15]

It was the focus of idol-worship by the beardless Indians of Outaouac County. They and other regional native peoples, like the Menomonie, still preserve oral traditions of the Memo-govis-si-oois, their name for the ancient copper miners. These "Marine Men" are described as bearded white foreigners, who arrived from their distant homeland far across the "Sunrise Sea" (Atlantic Ocean). They "committed sacrilege" against the Earth Mother by wounding her and digging out her "shiny bones." Some Indians who had been "corrupted" by the alien Memo-govis-si-oois assisted as laborers. DuTemple discovered:

Indian legends make no mention of these mining operations, which were of a magnificence and a magnitude worthy of being included in the history of any race. The legends do mention that a white race was driven out far back in the Indians' history. The fact

that Indian legends indicate that pieces of copper were revered as "manitous" or gods would seem to prove that they were not the people who mined and used the copper industrially.[16]

Indeed, among the Attiwandetons there was a tradition that recalled how their ancestors decimated a "white people" and seized their lands and animals. The Attiwandetons were, it is true, infamous for their depredations against fellow Indians, the Iroquois and Hurons, during the mid-1600s. Coincidentally, the Chippewas know a virtually identical account of a "white-skinned tribe" annihilated in the deep past.

Michigan's ancient copper enterprise poses a five-fold enigma: (1) Who were the miners? (2) Where did they come from? (3) What became of them? (4) What happened to the 500,000 tons (at least) of copper they removed? And (5) How did they find it in the first place? DuTemple observed in 1962, "Where this copper went is still a mystery."[17]

Twenty years later, Dr. James Scherz, professor of Civil Engineering at the University of Wisconsin (Madison), asked:

One of the basic questions that hasn't been answered yet is, "Where did all the copper from Lake Superior go?" All of the copper found in the mounds, although of a large amount, is but a small percentage of that mined. The Europeans have a complimentary problem. Where did all their copper come from? The Europeans were in a copper trading frenzy from 3000 to 1200 B.C., like we are now about oil, because copper drove their economy.[18]

Rudolf estimates that a typical Old World army of 100,000 infantry, outfitted with helmets, breastplates, shields, swords, daggers, spears and shin-guards, required 2,500 tons of copper (combined with substantially lesser amounts of tin and zinc to produce bronze).[19] Considering the vast amounts of bronze used by every high culture in the Homeric world, the manufacture of this strong, resilient metal was stupendous. The armies of Troy and Mykenaean Greece; the millions of tools used by Egyptian craftsmen to build the greatest temples and palaces of all time; the walls of Babylon sheeted in bronze, and thousands of bronze statues cast throughout the shores and islands of the Mediterranean—all demanded prodigious quantities of high-grade copper, which did not exist in anything approaching sufficient measure throughout Europe and the Near East. DuTemple noted that:

[T]he magnitude of the operation (in prehistoric Michigan) would indicate a strong metallurgically oriented culture. There was undoubtedly a great economic demand to support this operation with men, material, food and transportation. Such effort was probably not put forth for trinkets and ornaments, but rather for working tools, probably for armaments and to exchange in trade.[20]

The white-skinned Memo-govis-si-oois copper miners described in Indian traditions were said to have discovered the ore-bearing veins by throwing magical stones, called *yuwipi*, on the ground, which made the copper-rich rocks "ring, as brass does." Remarkably, the Menomonie account appears to conform to or at least suggest a prospecting technique actually practiced by European miners more than 3,000 years ago. Bronze with a high tin content (from one part in four to one in six or seven) emits a full, resonant tone when struck with a stone. Such bronze is today known as "bell metal" for the ringing sound it produces. To the Menomonie ancestors, the native copper and manufactured bronze, of which they knew nothing, must have seemed one and the same. When they saw the bronze being struck with a stone by the Marine Men to test its quality by the chime-sound it made, they assumed the copper had been magically transformed by the yuwipi.

A comparison of dates for Michigan's copper mining with events in the Old World underscores the overseas identity of the "Marine Men." The mining, as noted above, began around 3000 B.C. The turn of the fourth millennium witnessed the birth of the so-called "bronze age" in the Near East. Old World bronze production reached its zenith during the 13th century B.C., just when Michigan copper mining attained its maximum output. So too, the European bronze age ended abruptly around 1200 B.C., precisely the same narrow period in which the Great Lakes mines were suddenly abandoned. Such comparisons become particularly close when we learn that, along with copper, tin—that other component in the production of bronze—was likewise extracted from upper Michigan by the "Marine Men."

For the kingdoms of the Old World, copper was the nuclear fusion of their day. Without it, they were mineralogically and therefore technologically inferior to their enemies. But they lacked sufficient natural deposits. Michigan possesses the highest grade copper on Earth, and in the greatest abundance. Probably sometime during the late fourth millennium, European mariners landed along the eastern shores of North America. Asking after the numerous copper ornaments worn by the natives, the visitors were directed to Michigan's Upper Peninsula, where the veins were found and mining soon after began. Over the next 18 centuries, the mines expanded to meet the burgeoning demands of Old World cultures. But around 1200, the Homeric age was abruptly replaced by a dark one that was to last for the next 500 years, blotting out all memory of the overseas copper source. Meanwhile, in the mining region of North America's upper Great

Lakes, the European "Marine Men" were suddenly stranded and faced by the overwhelming numbers of a hostile native population that eventually exterminated them.

Perhaps the real mystery of the ancient copper miners is not their identity or even their fate, because a profusion of evidence has long told of who and what they were, and even what became of them. The enigma lies instead with our country's academic and educational establishments, which have for so long smothered all knowledge of American prehistory in the same dark ages that first veiled it, more than 3,000 years ago. ❖

FOOTNOTES

1 "Historical and Geological Record of the Copper Country," by Fred Rydholm, *Ancient American*, Vol. 5, No. 35, September/October, 2000.

2 "Michigan's Most Ancient Industry: The Prehistoric Mines and Miners of Isle Royale," by William P.F. Furgeson, in *Ancient Copper Mines of Upper Michigan*, by Octave DuTemple, Barrel, MI: Marlin Press, 1962, 54.

3 *Ancient Copper Mines of Upper Michigan*, by Octave DuTemple, Barrel, MI: Marlin Press, 1962, 12.

4 "Ancient Copper Mines of Isle Royale," by N.H. Winchell, *The Engineering and Mining Journal*, No. 32, December, 1881, 102.

5 "The Ancient Copper Mines of Isle Royale," by Jacob Houghton, in *Ancient Copper Mines of Upper Michigan*, by Octave DuTemple, Barrel, MI: Marlin Press, 1962, 82.

6 "Prehistoric Mining in the Copper Country," by Roy W. Direr, in *Ancient Copper Mines of Upper Michigan*, by Octave DuTemple, Barrel, MI: Marlin Press, 1962, 73.

7 *Ibid.*, 76.

8 "Letters to the Editor," John H. Rudolf, *Ancient American*, Vol. 5, No. 36, November/December, 2000, 18, 19.

9 "Who Mined Great Lakes Copper 4,000 Years Ago?" by Jim Grimes, *Ancient American*, Vol. 5, No. 35, September/October, 2000, 28.

10 *Ancient Copper Mines of Upper Michigan*, by Octave DuTemple, Barrel, MI: Marlin Press, 1962, 21.

11 "Ancient Aztalan," by S.A. Barrett, in the *Bulletin of the Public Museum of the City of Milwaukee*, No. 13, 1933, 56.

12 "Historical Sketch of the Lake Superior Copper District," *Mining Gazette*, Lansing, Michigan College of Mining and Technology, September 7, 1929.

13 "The First Copper Miners," by Jack Parker, *Compressed Air Magazine*, January, 1975, 8.

14 "The Ancient Copper Miners of Lake Superior," by Jacob Houghton, in *Ancient Copper Mines of Upper Michigan*, by Octave DuTemple, Barrel, MI: Marlin Press, 1962, 81.

15 "The Indians of North America," by Edna Kenton, elected and edited from *The Jesuit Relations and Allied Documents*, NY: Harcourt, Brace and Co., 1927, 123.

16 *Ancient Copper Mines of Upper Michigan*, by Octave DuTemple, Barrel, MI: Marlin Press, 1962, 14.

17 *Ibid.*

18 Quoted by Jerry Ambelang in "Aztalan: U.S. Stonehenge?" *The Capital Times*, Madison, WI, December 22, 1986.

19 "Letters to the Editor," John H. Rudolf, *op. cit.*

20 *Ancient Copper Mines of Upper Michigan*, by Octave DuTemple, Barrel, MI: Marlin Press, 1962, 19.

BIBLIOGRAPHY

Bailey, James, *The God-Kings and the Titans*, NY: St.Martin's Press, 1973.

Benedict, C. Harry, *Red Metal*, Ann Arbor: University of Michigan Press, 1958.

DuTemple, Octave, *Ancient Copper Mines of Upper Michigan*, Barrel, MI: Marlin Press, 1962.

Joseph, Frank, *Atlantis in Wisconsin*, Lakeville, MN: Galde Press, Inc., 1995.

Langford, George E., *Native American Legends*, NY: Doubleday & Co., 1961.

Murdock, Angus, *Boom Copper*, NY: The MacMillan Co., 1943.

Sodders, Betty, *Michigan Prehistory Mysteries*, Colfax, WI: Ancient American Publishers, 2001 reprint of the 1991 original.

Frank Joseph was for many years the associate editor of The Ancient American, *a magazine dedicated to mysteries of the Americas. He has written dozens of books on ancient mysteries, Atlantis, Lemuria and other topics of related interest to readers.*

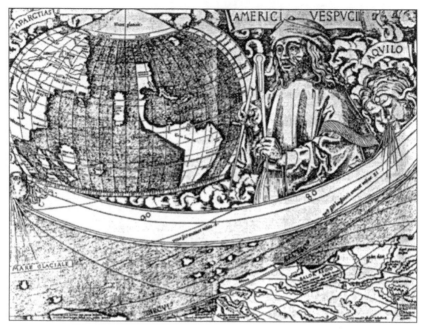

*Martin Waldseemuller published this map inset as part of an atlas in 1507.
The map is intended to show Vespucci's so-called "New World" discoveries as
being separate from Asia. Note that Vespucci's map erroneously shows a huge
sea separating Newfoundland from the truncated eastern coast and Florida—
suggesting that Vespucci did not have access to the latest Portuguese reports
indicating a solid coastline from Newfoundland to Brazil. His Asian coast is
merely a duplication of the bogus coast from Martin Behaim's globe of 1492—
showing that he was not aware of the latest Portuguese intelligence in this region either. Even his South American coast has numerous inaccuracies that
deviate from the Portuguese Padrao of 1502 (as evidenced by the Cantino
map). While Vespucci deserves credit for popularizing the concept of a "New
World," it appears that he merely copied preexisting Portuguese maps. (Photo
of map in the New York Public Library.)*

HOW THE PORTUGUESE MISLED CHRISTOPHER COLUMBUS

BY GUNNAR THOMPSON

In the late 15th century, Lisbon was the center of Europe's oceanic expansion. The explorations of the African coast, culminating in the rounding of the southern tip of the Dark Continent, are best known to historians. It gave Portugal access to the silks and spices of the Indies. But I suggest it is possible that much other exploration went on that is not so well documented—indeed, that Portugal secretly explored and mapped the coastline of the New World, and then used this information to thwart its No. 1 rival, Spain.

Ever since the days when Christopher Columbus set sail for Asia in 1492, historians have pondered over a legacy of misnamed continents, vanishing isles and ephemeral "straits" leading to the Promised Land. Columbus can be credited with launching "an Era of Confusion" by misnaming Cuba as the "Zaiton" peninsula that Marco Polo had visited on his trip to China in 1375. He subsequently confused Haiti with Japan; and he misnamed the native peoples because he thought they were living in India. Perhaps his biggest blunder was thinking that mainland south of Cuba was the biblical paradise of Adam and Eve.

These early misidentifications of lands we call "the Americas" came about largely as a result of the Spanish mariner's reliance upon bogus Portuguese maps. A reassessment of historical documents has finally exposed the overwhelming success of a grand Portuguese scheme to mislead commercial rivals. Loyal agents prepared a smorgasbord of deception that included fake maps, secret expeditions and unwitting accomplices who led competing nations down mistaken pathways to glory. A succession of heroic figures—including Columbus, the Cabots, Amerigo Vespucci, Magellan, Cortes and Giovanni Verrazano—played unwitting roles in Portuguese deception. They all knew just enough about world geography and Portuguese "secrets" to persuade royal patrons to invest in their heroic exploits. In the process, they managed to squander enormous amounts of money, men and materials in vain efforts to find elusive "shortcuts" to the wealth of the Indies.

Meanwhile, Portuguese mariners seem to have focused their attention on a laborious eastern route to the Orient by way of South Africa. It was not by accident that Portuguese navigators missed out on the fruitless efforts of their competitors to find a "western route" to Marco Polo's fabulous Cathay—the jewel of the Far East. Nearly lost to historians has been the record of Portuguese explorers who charted the western Atlantic Ocean in the early 15th century. This effort provided sufficient intelligence for Portuguese geographers to ascertain with great accuracy the coastlines of wilderness mainland (the Americas) from Newfoundland to Brazil. Having thus identified the location of "New World" continents across the seas, they began to lay the groundwork for the world's greatest coup of commercial espionage.

Instead of announcing the discovery of new lands in the west, Portuguese agents pretended that expeditions beyond the Azores had only found steppingstones on the way to Asia. They carefully recorded a secret mainland on the king's private map called the

THE DEVIRGA MAP

Fig. 1. The DeVirga Map features two new continents. A northwestern continent (I) includes a macro-peninsula (II—Florida) and huge gulf (Gulf of Mexico); southwest of Asia is an early version of Peru (III). DeVirga's northwestern continent, called "Norveca" on this map, is most likely derived from a New World survey by English Franciscans 1330-1360. (This facsimile is based on a 1932 photograph in Lucerne subsequently published in Imago Mundi Supplement IV, A Review of Early Cartography, *Amsterdam: N. Israel, 1964; and Gunnar Thompson,* The Friar's Map of Ancient America: 1360 A.D., *Bellevue: Radiobookstore, 1996.)*

Padrao, while publishing bogus charts that showed the Orient a short distance west across the Atlantic Ocean. It took Portugal's rivals more than three decades before they finally abandoned the search for a western shortcut to the Orient. Premature papal endorsements that favored the Spaniards actually helped to validate the bogus geography and promote belief in the grand deception. Meanwhile, Portuguese mariners continued unhindered on their way to the Spice Islands via the only practical route—around the Cape of Good Hope.

Modern historical emphasis upon the Columbus voyage in 1492 has unfortunately served to distract our attention from the important achievements of earlier voyagers. The effort to produce an accurate, scientific account of the Western Isles can be traced back to the English friar-scientist Roger Bacon. The Oxford scholar was so frustrated by the entrenched ignorance he encountered in Christian academies that he sent a proposal for widespread curricular reforms to Pope Clement IV. The pope realized the importance of Bacon's proposal, yet he also realized the difficulties inherent in trying to get people to accept new ideas that threatened established quasi-religious beliefs. Thus, he instructed Fr. Bacon to enumerate his ideas in a secret memorandum.[1]

Bacon tried to follow the pope's instructions, but he found it difficult to conceal his writings from inquisitive superiors because his "condensed" manuscript, the *Opus Majus*, ran to several hundred pages. Bacon sent his Opus by secret courier to the pope's residence in 1265. Within a few months, the pope was dead from a sudden, mysterious stomach ailment; Bacon was thrown into ecclesiastical prison; and his writings were publicly repudiated as they were burned.

In spite of these misfortunes, the cause of science was not lost. Bacon had trusted friends at Oxford University who were more prudent than their outspoken mentor. Within a few years of the great scientist's death in 1293, Oxford deans had resurrected a hidden copy of the *Opus Majus*; and they set into motion one of Bacon's cherished dreams—the scientific mapping of the Western Isles.

William Rede and Simon Breden took center stage in their development of curricula for the instruction of cadres of Franciscan students in surveying and astronomical observation.[2] They also built a factory to manufacture the necessary scientific equipment (astrolabes) required for the project, and they produced almanacs of the Sun, Moon and planets. These efforts took place with the complete support of one of the most powerful monarchs to grace the throne of England—King Edward III.

Several sources serve to confirm that English friars actually sailed to the Americas before Columbus. Maps and historical accounts reveal that between 1330 and 1360, the friars succeeded in producing a map of the eastern coast from Newfoundland to Brazil. One example of the new accuracy of English surveying is seen in the Medici Atlas Map of Northern Europe published in 1351. The Medici Map shows Greenland for the first time in its accurate location with respect to longitude and latitude northwest of England.

During the late 16th century, historian Richard Hakluyt published several reports concerning early English colonies and explorations in the New World. One of these was an account of a Dutch journalist, Jacob Cnoyen, who met up with a Franciscan friar who had come from the Western Isles in 1364.[3] According to the friar, he had encountered an Oxford Franciscan, who was busy using an astrolabe to measure the lay of the land in "Dusky Norway." This Nordic province was identified as a forested land with a temperate climate, someplace west of Greenland. Such a landscape clearly evokes visions of Franciscan friars in Nova

MYTHS OF CHRISTOPHER COLUMBUS AND THE PILGRIMS' MAYFLOWER

C hristopher Columbus did not discover the mainland of America. He never even saw the American mainland. America was, however, discovered (or really rediscovered, since the Vikings and others had been here centuries earlier—even millennia earlier, in some cases) by John Cabot, sailing under the English flag, in 1497. Nevertheless, the established facts of discovery by such men as Leif Eriksson and John Cabot have failed to dispel the popular illusion of Columbus's so-called discovery of America.

Similar myths abound in history. For example, why do the 600 families who trace their descent from the *Mayflower's* passengers now constitute an American aristocracy of sorts? The reality of British settlement in America is that Jamestown and the Old Dominion of Virginia were established in 1607, 13 years before the *Mayflower* set sail.

Why do we see Puritans, who were built up after the Civil War as the so-called Pilgrim Fathers, depicted wearing Quaker garb? George Fox, the founder of the Society of Friends (Quakers), was not born until four years after the *Mayflower* voyage. The Quakers were tolerant and quietist—the Puritans were neither. Whiggery, however, which is closely allied to Puritanism, pretends to the virtue of tolerance. As C.H. Douglas put it in *The Policy of a Philosophy*: "That is where Whiggism is so successful in that it puts forward in moral form something which it is extraordinarily difficult to disentangle for its slyness, something which, in fact, it is not really aiming at, at all."

Pictured above: Christopher Columbus. No portraits of the famed but mysterious navigator Christopher Columbus were made during his lifetime (c. 1446-1506), and there is much doubt whether any of the hundreds of existing portraits has any authority as a likeness. According to the recorded pedigree of this picture, it was painted in 1519 (13 years after the death of Columbus) by Sebastiano del Piombo, one of the great Venetian artists of the Renaissance. The portrait is highly regarded, but, curiously, it is a portrait that is surely not a reliable likeness of Columbus.

Scotia or Newfoundland. But we do not need to bother with guessing: Hakluyt identified the region as "Norumbega"—the eastern coast of North America.

Hakluyt and his associate, John Dee, identified the leader of the mapping effort as a prominent Oxford mathematician, Nicholas of Lynn. Geoffrey Chaucer characterized Friar Nicholas as a wayward Franciscan in *The Canterbury Tales*. By the time he had reached old age, Nicholas had joined the Carmelite Order to please his patron, John of Gaunt. Chaucer praised Nicholas in later life as a "reverend clerk."

Hakluyt informs us that the title given to the Franciscan travelogue was the Inventio Fortunatae, which was presented to King Edward III circa 1360. The title can be translated as "Discovery of the Fortunate Islands." This is an obvious reference to the so-called "Fortunate Islands" of Roman legend that were supposedly located in the "farthest reaches of the Western Sea."

Among the geographical features mentioned in the Inventio were brazil wood forests, "magnetic isles" around the Magnetic North Pole, abandoned habitations of former European colonists and numerous forested isles with a warm climate. These were all situated far beyond Greenland and may have extended to Brazil—which was renowned for its brazilwood forests.

The document was well known to Bristol merchants. We have evidence in the form of a letter written in 1496 in which the merchant John Day extends his apology to a Spanish admiral (probably Columbus) for having momentarily lost track of said document, which the admiral had previously requested.[1] Two Columbus biographers, Bartolomé de Las Casas and the admiral's son, Ferdinand, mentioned that Columbus had seen the Inventio and that it had played an important role in his research into isles situated west of Europe. Several cartographers, including Mercator, Ortelius and Abraham Judaeus, also mentioned their debt to the Inventio for depiction of the polar regions on their maps. These portrayals actually conform to ancient Roman legends about a huge magnetic mountain at the North Pole. Unfortunately, they served to mislead historians into assuming that the travelogue was merely the idle concoction of fantasy.

English scholars mounted a serious effort to locate the Inventio and a corresponding map in the 1580s—but to no avail. It was not until 1995 that researchers discovered a copy of the lost map nearly hidden away in the margins of an antique map found in Croatia.[5] The map in question, Fig. 1 (see page 43), is a Venetian world map that Albertin DeVirga compiled in 1414 (or 1411). De-Virga's map (authenticated by Von Wiser in 1912) includes two extra continents. The northwestern continent reaching out from the coast of Norway bears the caption: "Norveca." This is a variation of the name for Norway (Norbegia). On this map, Norveca probably represents a huge overseas province (Dusky Norway) that King Haakon IV of Norway-Sweden annexed in 1261. Another name for this province was "Landanu" or "New Land." According to Icelandic sagas, this new land was situated southwest of Iceland—suggesting mainland in the region of Nova Scotia or Newfoundland.

The most distinguishing feature of the Norveca continent is a macro-peninsula that reaches out above a huge gulf. This is the first example in a long series of maps showing a similar geographical area across the Atlantic Ocean from Europe. Over time, Portuguese cartographers steadily moved this gulf and macro-peninsula toward the south on a series of subsequent maps until they assumed the exact positions of Florida, the Gulf of Mexico and Brazil. It is probably not a coincidence that this corresponds to the same region that early writers indicated as being visited by Franciscan surveyors.

Modern historians missed out on the significance of DeVirga's map and the following series of Florida maps due to a mistaken assumption that maps of the New World could not possibly pre-date the Columbus voyage of 1492.

The traditional story of Portuguese Atlantic exploration tends to focus attention upon mariners who blazed a trail of colonies down the west coast of Africa under the direction of Prince Henry the Navigator (1420-1460). It would seem from this itinerary of African conquest that the Portuguese became obsessed with establishing an eastern sea route to the Orient from the very outset of maritime exploration. Virtually lost to public awareness is the tremendous effort that Portuguese mariners invested in the Western Atlantic.

As the great-grandson of England's King Edward III and the grandson of John of Gaunt (patron of Friar Nicholas of Lynn), Prince Henry was in a position to inherit the navigational secrets of the Oxford Franciscans. In 1420, he must have already known the approximate location of mainland west of Europe. Thus, it was no accident that early in the course of his stewardship, Prince Henry dispatched numerous explorers to seek the location of mainland referred to as "Antillia" or the "Isle of Seven Cities."[6]

Among these Lusitanian navigators were Goncalo Cabral, Joao Fernandes, Vincent Dias, Diego de Tieve, Dom Fernao, Joao Vogado, Joao Vaz Corte-Real and sons, Ruy Concalves, Fernao Telles, Joao Affonso de Estreito, Alonso DeHuelva, Fernao Dulmo, Jacobus Carnus, Joao Coelho and Martin Behaim—to name a few. For details of Portuguese Atlantic explorations see Henry Harrisse, *The Discovery of North America*, 1892; Thompson, 1996, 175-244.

"Antillia" is the name of a mid-Atlantic isle that shows up on early 15th-century Portuguese maps. The name endured on 16th-century maps and was eventually applied to the Caribbean Islands we generally call "the Greater Antilles"—Cuba, Haiti and Puerto Rico.

According to legends recounted by Ferdinand Colon and summarized in captions on the Behaim Globe of 1492 and the Ruysch Map of 1508, Antillia was a place of refuge for Christians who fled the Saracen invasion of Portugal in A.D. 714. The 16th-century Spanish historian Antonio Galvano identified the Antilles as being equivalent to the "new isles" that Spain claimed following the Columbus expedition.[7] Ferdinand Colon mentioned that Antillia was situated 200 leagues (or about 600 miles) west of the Azores. Some writers such as William Babcock and Karre Prytz regard Antillia as an early representation for the eastern coast of North America.[8] Most historians have relegated Antillia to the trash heap of "fantasy isles" found along the fringes of medieval maps.[9]

The name "Antillia" is variously interpreted as having one of the following meanings: (1) an isle "ante" or in front of Europe; (2) an isle "opposite" Tile—which was an old Roman name for Iceland (thus, ant-tile); or (3) the "ancient isle" derived from the word *antiglia*. The last version occurred on some 16th-century maps as an alternative name for the Antipodes (aka Mundus Novus or South America).[10]

One Portuguese chart by the Venetian cartographer Andrea Bianco clearly shows that secret mariners had located and charted the coast of Florida by 1436. This chart portrays the distinct outline of a macro-peninsula in the shape of Florida attached to a conventionalized rectilinear island. A caption on Bianco's chart indicates that this isle is called "Antillia" and that it is located beyond the Sargasso Sea in the far-western Atlantic Ocean. This chart suggests that Antillia was regarded as a huge isle of possibly continental dimensions that was separate from Asia. It served as the prototype of a land area that eventually became identified as Florida.

Another Bianco chart from this time period assures us that the

Portuguese had determined the location of Brazil by 1448. Bianco's chart shows land 3,000 miles southwest of Africa with the caption "isle authenticated." This is the approximate location of Brazil on early 15th-century maps. Use of the term "authenticated" instead of "discovered" suggests that the map documents an expedition sent to confirm the existence of a place that was previously sighted.

Although modern historians continue to argue over the significance of Portuguese expeditions farther west, there are numerous testimonials indicating that Portuguese mariners succeeded in charting the coast of the North American shoreline opposite Europe. The biographer of Columbus, Ferdinand Colon, wrote that the Portuguese had succeeded in reaching Antillia by 1430.[11] The Martin Behaim Globe includes a caption indicating that European ships had passed by Antillia in 1414; and the 16th-century historian Antonio Galvano mentioned an ancient Portuguese report that a ship had landed at Antillia in 1447.[12] Furthermore, maps from this era of exploration in the western Atlantic confirm that the Portuguese succeeded in accurately charting the New World.

Charts made by cartographers working under royal appointments confirm the increasing exactitude with which Portuguese navigators determined the location of the overseas mainland. A summary of the coordinates from these maps is presented in Table 1 (see page 61).

By the time that the Venetian cartographer Andrea Bianco made his world map and Atlantic chart in 1436, the macro-peninsula was shown to be fairly close to the actual location of Florida—only 7 degrees too far north and about 1,000 miles too far east.

Fra Mauro, who worked with Bianco in Venice, was commissioned to make a map for the king of Portugal in 1459. His map placed the macro-peninsula at 25 degrees N—right on the mark for Florida, although the design of his map prevents the estimation of longitude.

Paolo Toscanelli was a Florentine cartographer who sent a letter and map to King Alphonso V of Portugal in 1474. His letter suggested the possibility of a westward voyage to the Orient directly across the Atlantic Ocean. He indicated that the "Zaiton" peninsula of Asia extended down to about 20 degrees, some 4,500 miles west of Europe.

About the year 1480, the German cartographer-astrologer Martin Behaim arrived in Lisbon. He is said to have brought along new instruments which enabled more meticulous calculations of the conjunctions of celestial objects. He was a pupil of Regiomontanus, whose student, Bernard Walther, is credited with using a clock driven by weights that enabled calculation of celestial phenomena that was accurate to one minute.[13] Previously, astronomers were limited to vague calculations based upon the inherent uncertainties of sundials, candles and water clocks. From this point on, we see evidence of increasing accuracy with respect to Portuguese calculations of longitude and latitude. For this achievement, King John awarded Behaim with knighthood in 1484.

Henricus Martellus and Martin Behaim (colleagues from Nuremberg) placed the southern tip of the macro-peninsula on their maps at the Tropic of Cancer (23 degrees 27'N) or just a bit south of the actual latitude of Florida. Their highly similar maps (from 1489-1492) confirm that Portuguese mariners had determined the actual latitude for the macro-peninsula (Florida) with its tip just above the Tropic of Cancer. It seems that Martellus and Behaim erred by approximately 200-500 miles in their estimates of the longitudinal distance between Europe and the western mainland.

According to most historians, medieval Europeans were completely ignorant of both the Asian coast and the North American coast—so there is no authoritative explanation for why cartographers should have elected to portray such a macro-peninsula across from Europe. If we examine the locations given for the macro-peninsula on a temporal basis, we can determine that successive cartographers elected to move the southeastern tip of the macro-peninsula steadily toward the actual coordinates of Florida. Since these cartographic adjustments occur during a period of known Portuguese explorations in the western Atlantic, it seems apparent that the Portuguese had accurately determined the location of mainland (Florida or Antillia) prior to the Columbus expedition.

Throughout the literature dealing with the Age of Discovery, we are reminded that "Spain and Portugal classified their voyages as state secrets."[14] In Portugal, the most carefully guarded geographical secret was the official *Padrao* or "King's Map," which included all the latest intelligence from around the world. This map was so secret that even Portuguese explorers knew the latest charts only from their own small region of the world. Only the king and his closest advisors had access to the one map that gave the whole picture of the world.

Columbus was aware that the Portuguese had the best intelligence regarding world exploration. However, as a foreigner and a commoner, he had little chance of gaining access to Portuguese royal secrets. He tried other methods to learn what he could from the masters. Thus he volunteered to accompany expeditions to the coast of Africa and beyond Iceland, where he sailed in 1477. He worked with his brother (or uncle) at a map shop in Lisbon for several years, and he associated with Martin Behaim, a German expatriate, who was among the most knowledgeable of Portuguese cartographers.[15]

Columbus revealed his familiarity with Behaim by mentioning his name in a letter written to support the proposal of sailing west to the Orient.[16] It hardly seems coincidental that he shared the same geographical concepts as Behaim and Martellus with respect to the circumference of Earth (20,000 miles), the length of a degree (56.66 miles), and the approximate distance across the Atlantic to Japan and the Orient (some 3,000-4,000 miles).

Ultimately, the Portuguese maps and rumors of successful voyages to distant isles convinced Columbus (and many others) that a westward trip to the Orient was feasible.[17]

In fact, it was because he had a Portuguese map that he even risked the venture in the first place. Although the actual map that Columbus used on his voyage has not survived, historians are fairly confident that they know what it looked like. Presumably, it was some variation of late 15th-century charts like those that Martellus and Behaim circulated in public—seemingly in blatant disregard of the Portuguese policy of secrecy.

Historian Zvi Dor Ner observed that:

The 20-inch globe constructed at Nuremberg by Martin Behaim represented the last, best attempt at understanding the distributions of land and water on the earth before Columbus set out upon his enterprise. Behaim's globe, in fact, showed the world as Columbus believed it to be.[18]

According to historian Kenneth Nebenzahl: "Columbus himself could find no better map (than the one by Martellus) to show him the way to Asia."[19] It mattered not whether Columbus followed a map by Behaim, Martellus, or Toscanelli—as they all repeated the same kind of bogus geography. None of the maps actually showed what was in the *Padrao*. Behaim was particularly deceptive: his map did not even show the new mainland (Brazil) that he had found on a recent voyage south of the equator.

Columbus, of course, found land precisely where it was indicated on his maps. Thus, he was convinced that his maps were accurate and that he had indeed reached the coast of India. In his log entry for October 24, 1492, Columbus wrote that: "All my globes and world maps seem to indicate that the island of Cipangu is in this vicinity."[20] A few days later, he surmised that he had somehow passed by Cipangu only to reach mainland. On November 2, he wrote: "I have calculated that I have come 1,142 leagues (3,426 miles) from the island of Hierro in the Canaries. I am certain that this is the mainland."[21] Considering that Columbus had estimated the length of a voyage to mainland Asia at about 3,600 miles prior to his voyage using Portuguese charts, his discovery of land within 200 miles of his estimate is nothing less than remarkable—unless his map was exceptionally accurate to begin with.

Modern historians have had a dickens of a time trying to reconcile the accuracy of land areas on Portuguese maps with their conviction that the existence of land where Columbus expected to find it was a fortuitous "coincidence." Thus, the traditional story of the Columbus voyage begins with an enigma—the map that should not exist.

F ew historians have ventured an explanation for why Portuguese mariners sailing toward the Spice Islands apparently chose the long route around the Cape of Good Hope. Meanwhile, all the published maps by their leading cartographers clearly showed that the shortest route by far (4,000 miles vs 15,000 miles) was directly west across the Atlantic. Of course, the reason why the Portuguese did not follow the easy route indicated by their own maps was due to the inherent inaccuracy of charts designed to confuse commercial rivals.

Columbus must have suspected that something was amiss

when he stopped by the castle of King John II on his way back to Spain in 1493. Instead of acknowledging the success of the Columbus enterprise, King John informed Columbus that the isles he had found in the Caribbean region were already known to the Portuguese as "Antillia." The king's chronicler, Ruy de Piña, recorded that the Spanish mariner believed he had reached Cipangu and the Asian mainland—but he had actually arrived at Antillia.[22] Historian Peter Martyr also concluded that Columbus had reached isles previously known as "the Antilles":

> **He (Columbus) assumed that he had found Ophir, whither Solomon's ships sailed for gold, but the descriptions of the cosmographers well considered, it seems that both these and the other islands adjoining are the islands of Antillia.**[23]

King John added further insult to his Spanish guest by informing him that a new continent was situated south of the Antilles. This was a reference to Brazil—whose mainland had been known to the Portuguese at least by the time of Andrea Bianco's map in 1448—yet it did not appear on any public maps. Martin Behaim had even sailed there sometime before 1490, according to a passage in Shedel's Chronicle, but the mainland did not appear on the globe he put on display in Nuremberg.[24]

Columbus eventually made a voyage to the southern mainland in 1498 in order to ascertain what the king of Portugal had meant by a "new mainland" in that direction. Ironically, most historians designate 1498 as the "official" discovery of New World mainland by Columbus—in spite of the fact that Brazil was already shown on secret Portuguese maps. Cabral's "official" discovery did not occur until the year 1500.

Columbus was certain that the Portuguese were trying to protect some vital secret, which he presumed might be the location of King Solomon's gold mines located in the biblical isle of Ophir. It seems apparent from subsequent events that the vital secret they wanted to preserve was actually their lucrative sea-route to the Spice Islands.

Upon reaching Spain, Columbus declared the success of his mission. He arrived before his patrons, Ferdinand and Isabella, at the head of a parade that he had hired as a marketing gimmick. It worked. The sovereigns got so wrapped up in the festive atmosphere that they promptly dispatched an emissary to Pope Alexander VI with the good news. They also requested spiritual endorsement for their commercial and evangelical mission to China. The pope concurred by issuing a bull giving Spain a monopoly over maritime expeditions west of a line 100 leagues beyond the Canary Islands. This declaration threatened Portuguese access to Brazil—although it established a doctrine that protected their African colonies and seaways from competition.

Portugal threatened to go to war in order to protect access to Brazil and the valuable resources of brazilwood, slaves and gold that were known to be present. Spain promptly acquiesced in the Treaty of Tordesillas in 1494. The line of demarcation was redrawn 370 leagues west of the Canary Islands, thereby giving Portugal access to Brazil. An English spy, Robert Thorne, informed King Henry VII in 1527 that prior to Columbus's voyage: "The king of Portugal had already discovered certain islands that lie against Cape Verde and also a certain part of the mainland toward the south and called it the land of Brazil."[25]

The plot had been a great success. For the next three decades, Portugal's commercial rivals would nearly exhaust their maritime resources attempting to first locate and then penetrate the New World mainland in a desperate effort to find a non-existent shortcut to the riches of the Orient.

Public exposure of the Portuguese secret of a New World mainland finally came about in 1502 with the publication of Amerigo Vespucci's *Mundus Novus* letter. According to the Florentine explorer who had traveled under both Spanish and Portuguese flags, there was a hitherto-unknown mainland or "New World" south of the equator. Since the report that Columbus filed on his 1498 voyage to the southern continent had not been published, Vespucci's document took precedence as a scientific achievement. It was the first public disclosure of a whole new continent, separate from Asia, that promised vast opportunities and resources for Europeans. Based on this revelation, the German mapmaker Martin Waldseemuller elected to honor Vespucci by christening the new southern continent with the name "America."

Yet even this announcement proves to have been deceptive. The only cartographic evidence that seems to have come forth from Vespucci to substantiate his claim of finding a "New World" was published along with Waldseemuller's Atlas in 1507. This map is merely a crude copy of Portuguese charts that were already in existence. Vespucci had access to a limited selection of Portugal's New World maps during his service as a minor navigator. He had the good fortune of discovering a new way to measure longitude using the conjunction of planets with the Moon. This knowledge enabled him to estimate the circumference of the Earth within a few miles of its actual distance—adding some 4,500 miles to the current estimate—and providing room on his map for a New World just east of Asia across a narrow ocean. He did not know that secret voyages of the Corte-Real brothers had confirmed continuous shoreline from the Bacallaos (Newfoundland) to Brazil. Thus, his own chart, which was very popular in Europe, indicated the presence of a non-existent Northwest Passage to the Orient.

Shortly after Vespucci's return in October of 1502, a secret agent, working for an Italian duke, managed to purchase a copy of the ultra-secret *Padrao* from an anonymous traitor. Albert Cantino's Map is the only copy of the *Padrao* known to have survived—although several subsequent charts (Canerio's Map—1505; and Waldseemuller's Carta Marina—1516) seem to have been based upon a similar Portuguese original.

Cantino's Map includes the earliest European navigational charts of the coast of Asia obtained by Pero de Covilha (circa 1487) and Vasco Da Gama (1498). This is the earliest extant map to show the New World mainland as being totally separate from Asia. Indeed, the Asian coast is shown to extend all the way from below the equator to the Arctic Circle. Although the distance of the Asian mainland west of the New World is not indicated on this map, it is indicated on Waldseemuller's Carta Marina—which is a virtually identical map published in 1516 under the title "A Portuguese Navigational Sea Chart of the Known Earth and Oceans." From this map, we can deduce that the Portuguese had already determined that the Asian coast was some 160 degrees or about 9,600 miles farther west than the Columbus landfall.

Since the theft of the *Padrao* map (aka Cantino map) was not made public, there was no way for most Europeans to realize that the Portuguese had preceded Vespucci in determining the existence of a New World. Furthermore, the map did not include longitude, nor did it include the latest information from the Corte-Real expeditions (showing a continuous coastline from Newfoundland to Brazil). We are left with the impression that the theft of the *Padrao* did not compromise Portuguese secrets, while Amerigo Vespucci's concept of a "New World" was simply what Portuguese agents wanted him to reveal in their continuing effort to mislead commercial rivals. ❖

ENDNOTES:

1 For details about Roger Bacon's geographical proposals see Thompson, Gunnar, *The Friar's Map of Ancient America—1360 AD*, Bellevue, Radio Bookstore Press, 1996 (www. radiobookstore. com).

2 Austin Poole, *Medieval England*, Oxford: Clarendon Press,1958, 592-93.

3 See Richard Hakluyt, *Divers Voyages—Touching the Discoveries of America*, Ann Arbor: University Microfilms, 1966 (reprint from 1582); *Principal Navigations*, Toronto: Dent and Sons, 1909 (reprint from 1600); *Great and Rich Discoveries of the English Nation*, 1580.

4 Samuel E. Morison, *The European Discovery of America*, New York: Oxford Press, 1971, 206.

5 See Thompson, 1996; also "The Cantino Bridge from Antillia to America," *Information Bulletin of the Western Association of Map Libraries*, November 1999, 8-22.

6 Thompson, 1996, 175-244.

7 William Babcock, *Legendary Isles of the Atlantic*, American Geographical Society, 1922, 72. Antonio Galvano, The Discoveries of the World, Hakluyt Society Publications, 1st Series, Vol. 30, London, 1862, 72, identifies the Antilles with the isles that were later called "New Spain."

8 Babcock, 1922, 72-84, and Karre Prytz, *Westward Before Columbus*, Oslo, Maritime Forlag, 1991, are among the proponents of Antillia representing America. Babcock (153) visualizes Antillia as Cuba; Prytz believes that Antillia represents the North American coast from Florida to the Carolinas.

9 See for example Donald Johnson, *Phantom Islands of the Atlantic*, New York, Avon, 1994; Raymond Ramsey, *No Longer on the Map—Discovering Places that Never Were*, New York, Ballantine, 1972.

10 For an example of "antiglia" for South America see the Portolan Atlas of 1508, in Babcock, 1922, showing the Edgerton MS 2803 of the British Museum.

11 Babcock, 1922, 72 quotes Ferdinand Colon: "[I]n the time of Henry infant of Portugal (1430), a Portuguese ship was drove by stress of weather to this island Antillia."

12 Galvano, 1862, 72.

13 Lloyd A. Brown, *The Story of Maps*, New York: Bonanza Books, 1959, 211.

14 J.B. Harley, *Maps and the Columbus Encounter*, Milwaukee: Golda Meir Library, 1990, 75.

15 It is also likely that Columbus saw similar maps in the papers of his wife's family on the island of Madeira.

16 Samuel E. Morison, *Christopher Columbus*, New York: Heritage Press, 1963, 16.

17 See for example Robert H. Fuson, *The Log of Christopher Columbus*, Camden: International Marine, 1987, 25.

18 Dor Ner, *Christopher Columbus*, Washington, D.C.: National Geographic, 1991, 83. *f*

19 Kenneth Nebenzahl, *Atlas of Columbus and the Great Discoveries*, New York, Rand McNally, 1990, 13.

20 Dor Ner, 1991, 164. ["Cipangu" means Japan, which Columbus took to be part of India.—Ed.]

21 Dor Ner, 1991, 165.

22 Arthur Newton, *The Great Age of Discovery*, Freeport, NY, Books for Libraries, 1932, 94.

23 Pietro Martyr d'Anghiera, "The Decades of the New World or West India," in F.A. Mac-Nutt, trans., *The Eight Decades of Peter Marthy D'Anghera*, New York, 1912.

24 John Thatcher, *Christopher Columbus*, New York: AMS Press, 1967, 73, believes this is an error.

25 Jack Beeching, ed., Richard Hakluyt—*Voyages and Discoveries*, London, Penguin Books, 1972, 50.

BIBLIOGRAPHY:

Boxer, Charles R. *Four Centuries of Portuguese Expansion, 1415-1825: A Succinct Survey.* Johannesburg: Witwatersrand University Press, 1961.

Hart, Henry H. *Sea Road to the Indies: An Account of the Voyages and Exploits of the Portuguese Navigators,* together with the *Life and Times of the Dom Vasco da Gama,* Capitao-Mor, Viceroy of India and Count of Vidigueira. New York: Macmillan, 1950.

Morison, Samuel Eliot. *Portuguese Voyages to America in the Fifteenth Century.* Cambridge, Mass.: Harvard University Press, 1940. (Reprint: Octagon Books, 1965.)

Prestage, Edgar. *The Portuguese Pioneers.* London: A.& C. Black, 1933.

Table 1
Portuguese Macro-Peninsula/Antillia

Author/Map	Date	Source	Lat. N	Miles
Bianco (a)	1436	Ven./Port.	35 degrees	1,000
Bianco (b)	1436	Ven./Port.	30 degrees	3,000
Fra Mauro	1459	Ven./Port.	25 degrees	?
Toscanelli	1474	Flor./Port.	20 degrees	4,500
Martellus	1489	Ger./Flor.	23 degrees	4,000
Martellus	1490	Ger./Flor.	23 degrees	4,000
Behaim	1492	Ger./Port.	23 degrees	4,500
Florida	2001	Mod. Atlas	25 degrees	4,200

Key: Ven.=Venetian; Port.=Portuguese; Flor.=Florentine;
Ger.=German. (a) world map, (b) Atlantic chart.

Gunnar Thompson, born in Seattle in 1946, derives his interest in cultural diffusionism and pre-Columbian American civilizations from his childhood experiences in the northwest and his heritage of Norwegian, German and American Indian ancestors. A multi-talented artist, he is the author of American Discovery, Spirit Sign *and* Nu Sun: Asian-American Voyages 500 B.C., *as well as books on public policy, multinational economics and creative education.*

Water still flows in grooved channels leading to the sacred fountains of the prehistoric temple tomb of Tampu Machay in Peru. In the background notice the massive, polygonally-cut stone blocks characteristic of pre-Inca architecture.

THE MIND-BOGGLING ACCOMPLISHMENTS OF THE PRE-INCA CIVILIZATIONS

BY RALPH P. FORBES

According to court historians, the ancient civilizations of South America had no tools made of anything harder than wood, copper and stone. And even the Incas, the most recent of these civilizations (A.D. 1105-1572), had no form of writing, we are told—much less the civilizations that preceded the Incas. However, this writer maintains that there was indeed an ancient writing system—indeed, more than one—and the pre-Incas had the use of bronze, iron and even steel.

History records mass holocausts of truth by serial culture destroyers, the traditional enemies of the truth. Most famous is the burning of the ancient library of Alexandria. The least known, perhaps, are the sneaky book burnings of the 20th century. An excellent example is the rare volume, *The Ayar-Incas: Volume I, Monuments, Culture, and American Relationships* by Miles Poindexter, LL.D. Poindexter was a U.S. senator. But some of his life's most important work was as U.S. ambassador to Peru. Ironically, one of the suppressed truths revealed in this lost book is that the Incas, as well as the cultures that preceded them, were once literate. But sadly there came a time when a cultural "Bolshevik," not unlike the more recent "Shining Path" terrorists, wiped out literacy by fire and sword. Yet, despite that atrocity, and the ruthless suppression of historical truth by certain elements after the Spanish conquest, much more was generally known about the pre-Columbian Americas, both North and South, a century ago than today. This destruction of historical truth is no accident.

It was in the late 1960s that this writer discovered and eagerly devoured a yellowed copy of *Ayar-Incas* in a major library. A few years later, when this writer had more time, he tried to get a copy—alas, to no avail. It apparently had even disappeared from the shelves of the library where this writer first read it. For decades he searched. Not a trace in used bookstores, garage sales etc. Rare book finders could not even find a listing. Internet searches did not have a clue. It was as if this writer had imagined the whole thing. Then at last after almost three decades he was able to borrow a copy long enough to scan it into an OCR program.

There yet remain thousands of miles of South American "superhighways" traversing steep valleys, rugged mountains and raging rivers that would daunt the engineers of our continental interstates. Remnants of a vast agricultural system of irrigation, terracing and cultivation testify to a high culture. Yet, against all reason, the "high priests" of the prevailing view of history claim these great peoples had neither iron nor a written language.

One of the puzzling mysteries of Peru has always been connected with the tools with which the artisans of the megalithic age cut the stones which are fitted with such perfection into the incomparable masonry of the temples, forts and palaces of the Andes.

Did the same mystery culture who built megalithic sites around the globe also erect these menhirs at Tiahuanaco? Popular attention has been focused on the monolithic Gateway of the Sun (a solar calendar), but the extensive pre-Inca ruins (erected by the mysterious Aymaras) south of Lake Titicaca, almost 13,000 feet above sea level, include temples, pyramids, columns and megalithic stairways that rival any in the world.

The fortress of Sacsayhuaman, the high altar of Ollantaytambo, the ashlar temple of Pisac, the royal tomb and sacred wall of Machu Picchu, the convents and temple of the sun at Cuzco, though of a crude architectural plan, are constructed of masonry of such nicety and perfection as perhaps has never been excelled anywhere else in the world. The stones, some of them of colossal size, are cut and joined in a perfect and mortarless union as though they had been molded into the corresponding angles and curves. They are all shaped to their place in the curving, sloping or rectilinear walls as though they had been fitted together by some plastic material by a master mason who combined the talents of a mathematician and an artist.

It is obviously impossible that this work of super-art, which is at least equal to the best examples of the masonry of the Orient, of Greece or of modern times, could have been accomplished merely with stone tools. These blocks were undoubtedly cut with metal bits, tempered to a hard edge. Many bronze chisels have been found in the huacas, but these are said to be easily dulled when tested in rock-cutting. Some of these tools contained 94 parts of copper to six of tin. Emerald, one of the hardest of stones, obtained by the Peruvians in considerable quantities from the desert of Atacama in the south, as well as from Colombia, was carved with ease and precision by the Peruvians.

In the cataclysm of the conquest and subsequent exploitation of the Indians by the Spaniards, many native arts were undoubtedly lost; and processes of tempering bronze so as to produce a hard cutting edge, which may have been known to the Peruvians when their country was overrun by the Spanish adventurers, may have been concealed by them from their oppressors and subsequently lost.

The Peruvians were acquainted with alloys and are said to have hardened their bronze by the mixture of a small part of gold with copper and tin, producing an alloy called *chumpi*. Seventy-five percent of the world's supply of vanadium, one of the most effective ingredients for hardening steel, comes from Peru; but it is not known that the ancient Peruvians had any knowledge of its use.

However, the megalithic masonry of Peru was a lost art long before the arrival of the Spaniards. The matchless walls of Cuzco, even those that did not belong to the megalithic age, had been constructed in the flowering of an art which had long since, like other arts of the Peruvians, fallen into decay, as had the American race itself, not only in Peru but in many other parts of the hemisphere. In many places there were the remains of cultures in both North and South America of which the inhabitants of the country, at the time of the arrival of the Europeans, had no knowledge and sometimes not even a tradition.

Nearly everywhere, however, there existed the tradition of a superior white race who had brought an ancient culture and erected the great monuments. The well-preserved Peruvian tradition was that the stone structures at Quinoa and Huaytara had been built by bearded white men with iron tools. Like much of its culture, the white race itself had disappeared just as it had in India, Polynesia and China in varying degrees, notwithstanding the restrictions of caste established for its protection.

The purity of the ancient religion, its worship of an omnipotent, invisible and immortal god, as among the Jews, Hindus and Egyptians, was corrupted by the worship of idols and perverted by lust. Some trace of the white Ayars still survived in the noble castes, and the mixture of their blood can be seen even today among the locals.[1] The main features of the pre-Ayar social organization still preserved the marvelous industry of the people at the time of the Spanish conquest; but the race itself, its character, and its culture were in a state of decadence.

Native legends say that when the prince Huanacauri Pirua[2] was reigning, there was a system of writing, and also men very wise in the alphabet, who were called Amautas. These men taught students reading, writing and astronomy. As far as this writer has been able to learn, they wrote on the leaves of the plantain tree, known as *quilcas*, which they first dried.

The Amauta king, Titu Yupanqui Pachacuti, was defeated and killed in the pass of Vilcanota (La Raya) by invaders from the south, black men among them.[3] The Cuzco dynasty was overthrown, the kingdom of the Amautas overrun, much of the ancient culture lost, and the dark ages enveloped Peru for hundreds of years.

Centuries later, when the ancient religion, which had meanwhile been nurtured in the remote vastness of the Vilcapampa, was reestablished by the survivors of the Ayars, an effort was made to revive the art of writing; but a reactionary priest, true to certain types of the clerical party, persuaded the king to proscribe it, under penalty of death.

Tupac Cauri, Pachacuti VII,[4]

> . . . began to pull his forces together and to recover some cities and provinces, but, as the people obeyed him with so little certainty and as they were so greatly corrupted in the matter of religion and customs, he took steps to conquer them, because he said that if these people communicated with his own they would corrupt them with the great vices to which they had given themselves up like wild beasts. Therefore he tactfully sent messengers in all directions, asking the chiefs to put a stop to superstition and the adoration of the many gods and animals which they adored; and the outcome of this was but a slight mending of their ways and the slaying of the ambassadors.
>
> The king dissembled for the time being and made great sacrifices and appeals to Illatici Huira Cocha. One reply was that the cause of the pestilence had been the letters, and that no one ought to use them nor resuscitate them, for, from their employment, great harm would come. Therefore Tupac Cauri commanded by law that, under the

Explorers of the late 19th century stand in front of the imposing stone walls of Sacsayhuaman.

pain of death, no one should traffic in *quilcas*, which were the parchments and leaves of trees on which they used to write, nor should [anyone] use any sort of letters. They observed this oracular command with so much care that after this loss the Peruvians never used letters. And, because in later times a learned Amauta invented some characters, they burnt him alive, and so, from this time forth, they used threads and *quipus* [knotted strings serving as reminders of what was uttered].[5]

In the great convulsion and the degeneracy which followed the overthrow of Titu Upanqui, much of the ancient culture besides letters was no doubt lost, possibly including the perfection of the art of the prehistoric masonry and the knowledge of the tools by which it was wrought. The unfinished condition of some of the

greatest of the monuments, the scattered material along the Inclined Way at Ollantaytambo, the wild confusion and disorder of
the high place itself, tell of the sudden disaster which fell upon
the workmen, the precipitancy with which they dropped their
tools and fled or were slaughtered where they stood. It is not impossible that the ancient builders, whose works would never
have been believed possible but that their imperishable solidity
and excellence have preserved them as bodily evidence of an
achievement which otherwise all the archeologists would have
proved to be preposterous, had steel tools.

Pontesinos chronicles the tradition that in the reign of the Ayar
Tacco Capac,[6] Peru was invaded by giants who came by the
sea. Some of them settled at Huayatara and Quinoa in the highlands above Ica, and Montesinos repeats the tradition that they
completed some buildings, which they found begun, with the instruments of iron, that they had brought with them from their
own land.

The scouts of Ayar Tacco Capac also reported that "very large
and tall men" had landed in the north about Santa Elena "and
were ruling that land from Puerto Viejo [so called by the Spanish
chronicler of the tradition] and that the natives of it were fleeing
from them because they used their bodies so ill, and in my opinion it was not that they fled from the sin, for they themselves had
it also, but that they fled from the danger of the instrument with
which the giants took their lives." This reference is somewhat
enigmatic, but it would seem to refer to a weapon of metal, probably a sword or knife; and as bronze and copper had long been
known to the Peruvians, it must have been some new and dead-
lier blade, possibly steel, with which the giant invaders terrified
the Indians of the coast.

Prescott quotes Ondegardo and Herrera as saying that the Peruvians had no tools of iron or steel and reflects that:

[I]t is worthy of remark that the Egyptians, the Mexicans and Peruvians, in their march toward civilization, should never have detected the use of iron that lay around them in abundance.[7] Prescott was mistaken as to the Egyptians, and the question is not at all clear as to the Peruvians. The Iron Age in Egypt, Chaldea, Assyria and China reaches back to 4000 B.C. Iron was found in the great pyramids and a steel instrument in the tomb of Tut-ankh-Amen. In Etruria iron appears as early as 1300 B.C. Mungo Park found the natives of the Niger River country, who had never seen a white man, smelting iron ore and making weapons and tools of iron.

A.H. Verrill in excavations at Cocle, Panama, in deposits he estimates as thousands of years older than the Christian era, found "at a depth of 5 1/2 feet below the surface, at the temple site, among broken pottery and imbedded in charcoal . . . a steel or hardened iron implement. The greater portion is almost completely destroyed by corrosion but the chisel-shaped end is in good condition. It is so hard that it is scarcely touched by a file and will scratch glass."[8] With such a tool in the hands of the great Quiche or Quichua masons, the carving of the stone columns and idols which lay about its burial place at Cocle, or even the perfectly fitted masonry blocks in the smooth walls of Cuzco, would be explained.

Bourbourg[9] quotes Velasco as saying that:

[T]he Peruvians did not use iron, although they knew it under the name of *quillay*, because they knew how to temper copper like steel.[10] Mercurio Peruano[11] mentions the following mines as having

been worked by the Incas (or rather those who preceded them): Escamera, Chilleo and Abatanis, gold; Choquipina and Porco, silver; Curahuato, copper; Carabuco, lead; probably the neighborhood of Oruro, says Bollaert (*Antiquities*, 60), supplied tin; and the magnificent iron mines of Ancoriames on the east shore of Lake Titicaca. America is still to be discovered. It is necessary to remove the veil under which the Spanish policy has sought to cover her ancient civilization.[12]

But it seems likely that the making of steel, like letters, was a lost art when Pizarro arrived in Peru. Like the great race that worked the copper mines on Lake Michigan and built the dolmens and earthworks of the Mississippi valley, the masons of the Vilcanota were known only by their works.   ❖

ENDNOTES:

1 As to the white natives of Chachapoyas, see Cieza de Leon, *La Cronica del Peru* (Madrid, 1922), 259.

2 The third of the "proto-historic" kings of Cuzco, listed by Montesinos (Montesinos, Memorias Antiguas [Hak. Soc., London, 1920]). Means (note to Memorias Antiguas, xlvi) places his date at about A.D. 200. However, the beginning of the white Pirua-Ayar culture of southern Peru, represented by this legendary chief, was no doubt much earlier than the date given by Means.

3 The traditions state that the king, contrary to the advice of his officers, left his fortifications in the pass, which, properly defended, should have been impregnable; and went out to meet the invaders in the open. He sacrificed discretion and strategy to his personal bravery. (Montesinos, supra, 61.)

4 Seventy-eighth king of Ayar blood in Montesinos's list. Means, on Montesinos's data, calculates 1300 B.C. as the beginning of his reign. This event was long before the rise of the Inca dynasty, and no doubt was much earlier than the date mentioned.

5 Montesinos, supra, 64. The carefully preserved traditions of Peru, as given to the earliest Spanish chroniclers by the Quipucamayocs and Amautas; the trained recorders with *quipus*, or knotted cords, and the professional legend-bearers who preserved and passed on by word of mouth the story of the race from one generation to another, covered a period variously estimated by the chroniclers and later historians as from 2,000 to 3,000 years before the arrival of Pizarro in Peru; and yet none of these traditions undertook to account for the building of Sacsayhuaman, Tiahuanaco or Ollantaytambo. These megalithic works were older than tradition.

Besides the archaic migrations which brought corn, place names, racial names and descriptive words and structure of common speech from Mexico to Peru, and perhaps a movement of primitive man along the same lines from north to south even earlier than this, there appears to have been an archaic movement of the megalithic race from Asia to the Pacific islands and thence to the American continent. This migration, which no doubt consumed many centuries, has left its most striking monuments in the Carolines, in Easter Island, and in the Peruvian Andes. This culture was so old that neither the Polynesians nor the Peruvians at the time of their discovery by the Europeans had any knowledge of the builders of the megalithic structures.

In both Peru and Polynesia the trained minstrels and historians had preserved the chronicles of the people from very remote times. But neither on the islands nor on the continent did the memory of man, as preserved and perpetuated in these traditions, run far enough back to account for the quarrying and transportation of the immense stones over long distances, the Cyclopean masonry, or the art by which they had been carved and fitted with so much nicety, for the immense walls, harbors, palaces, temples and fortresses; nor for the origin or description of the race which had left these imperishable monuments of its power. Even today these stupendous structures seem rather the work of supermen, or demigods, than of men.

6 Given by Means (Int. to Montesinos, supra) as A.D. 275, but probably much earlier.

7 *Conquest of Peru*, I, 126.

8 "The Pompeii of Ancient America," *The World's Work*, January, 1927, 86.

9 Int. to *Popol Vuh*, ccxxiv.

10 "It is remarkable," says Molina, "that iron, which is universally supposed to have been unknown to the American natives, has a specific name in the Chilean language. It is called *panilgue* and the instruments which are made of it *claioquel*, to distinguish them from those made of other substances, which are comprised under the generic name *nulin*." *The Geographical, Natural and Civil History of Chile*, translated from the original Italian, etc., London, chap. iv.

11 Vol. 1 (1791), 201.

12 Popol Vuh, ccxxiv. "Iron-working was brought into the East Indian archipelago by the megalithic immigrants. The stone-using immigrants appear to have been people well acquainted with the working of gold, copper and iron. W.J. Perry, *Megalithic Culture of Indonesia* (Manchester, 1918), 178.

Ralph Forbes is a student of North and South American prehistory and Keltic culture. He resides in Arkansas and is a longtime leader in the populist movement. He was for years a bureau cguef at AMERICAN FREE PRESS *newspaper.*

Out-of-Place Finds in Maya Land

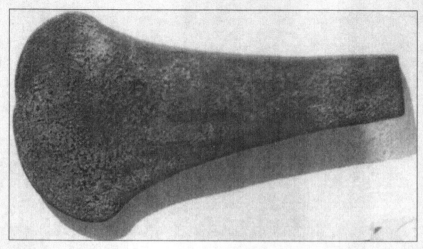

This bronze ax head was made in the eastern Mediterranean region, probably in what is today known as Palestine. Dating from about 1000 B.C., it was found at a Mayan archeological site on Cozumel Island, Mexico.

Displayed here is another bronze ax head, said to be of eastern Mediterranean origin. It was alleged to also have been found among some ruins on Cozumel Island.

EVIDENCE FOR MUSLIM POPULATIONS LIVING IN PRE-COLUMBIAN AMERICA

BY JOHN TIFFANY

There is compelling evidence that Muslims played an early role in the permanent settlement of what was eventually to become the United States and that they intermingled with the native inhabitants of the Americas. Here some of the evidence is presented backing up the theory that Muslims were in America before the Anglo-Saxons, and, in some cases, even before Christopher Columbus.

The early 17th-century Powhatan Indians' description of heaven is nearly word for word the description found in the Koran. Tennessee Gov. John Sevier records a 1784 encounter in what is now western North Carolina with a reddish-brown complexioned people supposed to be of Moorish descent who claimed to be Portuguese. In east Tennessee in the late 1700s Jonathan Swift, an Englishman, employed dark-skinned local men who were known as "Mecca Indians." These appear to correspond with the people we now call Melungeons.

The Melungeons, pushed off their lands, denied their rights, often murdered, always mistreated, became an embittered and nearly defeated people. Over the ensuing decades, in a vain effort to fit in with their "Anglo" neighbors, they lost their heritage, their culture, their names and their original religion but not their genetic structure.

Historical records document that from 1492 through the early 1600s an estimated 500,000 Jews and Muslims were exiled from Spain and Portugal through the Spanish Inquisition.

Hundreds of thousands of Muslim exiles escaped to ancestral homelands in Morocco, Algeria, Libya and Tunisia. The Barbary Coast pirates of north Africa sprang from this group. They, along with their Turkish compatriots, were renowned for their seagoing exploits as they sought revenge against the Spanish and Portuguese in ferocious Mediterranean sea battles.

Of course, they did not always win. Those pirates unfortunate enough to lose at sea often ended up as galley slaves beneath the creaking decks of Spanish and Portuguese ships bound for the New World. Other Muslims—Berbers in particular—Moriscos they were called—made their way to the Canary Islands, India, France and other countries. Interestingly enough, wherever these exiled Berbers went, they identified themselves as "Portuguese," even if they originated in Spain.

Finally, as the inquisitions grew in power and severity, even Christianized Moors and Jews were forced into exile. These "Conversos" (the name given to both Muslim and Jewish converts) were not really trusted by either the church or the Spanish government.

The Spanish Inquisition accomplished something of great historical value for Islam: There is little doubt that the Inquisition drove Spanish and Portuguese Muslims toward the New World.

While American schoolchildren learn of Columbus's role in the discovery of the New World, they are not told the entire story. Columbus employed both Moorish and Spanish sailors. On his fourth voyage in 1502 he records two important discoveries:

First, on the Caribbean island of Guadeloupe, he discovered an iron pot and an old ship's mast preserved in an Indian hut. He and his crew determined these artifacts had come from the Canary Islands. The Canaries, a Portuguese possession, had been a favorite dumping ground for Conversos of Muslim Berber origin.

Second, on July 31, 1502, came an even more extraordinary discovery. Off the island of Jamaica, Columbus encountered strange people on a strange ship that Western historians have generally considered to be Mayan Indians. This ship was 40 feet long with a diameter of eight feet and had a shaded pavilion in the center. From a distance, Columbus thought it to be uncannily like the Moorish galleys he had so often seen in the Mediterranean. There were approximately 40 men and women on the "galley," and, unlike the Jamaican Indians, these people wore clothing: sleeveless shirts and with showy colors and designs like those Columbus had seen in Muslim Granada.

These so-called Mayan Indians carried a cargo of tools, copper implements and forges for working copper. But perhaps Columbus's striking observation was that the women aboard this galley "covered their faces like the women of Granada." Were these truly Mayan Indians? Or is this simply one more case of biased historians refusing to accept the fact that Muslims could have reached the New World before Columbus?

In 1527, the first land crossing of the United States by a non-Indian most likely was achieved by Azemmouri, a Moroccan Berber, a Muslim. Originally he was a member of a Spanish expedition of 300 men. Only Azemmouri and three of his comrades survived this 11-year, 5,000 mile trek from Florida to the West Coast and back to Texas. He was the first known explorer from the Old World to enter a Pueblo Indian village, and the story of his daring exploits makes for fascinating reading. (It is not known if his three comrades were Muslims.)

The establishment of Jamestown, Virinia in 1607 was an important event in American history. But it was by no means the first European settlement in what today is the United States. The Spanish established a colony in what is now South Carolina in 1566, more than 40 years before Jamestown. The colony was known as Santa Elena. Ethnically, many of the Santa Elena colonists were Berbers, recruited by Capt. Juan Pardo (who himself was Portuguese). Santa Elena throve for more than 20 years, until it was overrun by the English in 1587. But since the English won the struggle for this land, Santa Elena is conveniently left out of the history books. History, as they say, is written by the victors.

Many of the Santa Elena colonists were converted Muslims and Jews or Conversos. When Santa Elena fell, its inhabitants—including its converted Jews and Muslims —escaped into the mountains of North Carolina. And there they survived, intermarrying with Indians and eventually merging with a second group of Muslims arriving on American shores in, ironically, 1587, the same year Santa Elena fell.

North African Berbers, Arabs and Turks captured in the Mediterranean by the Spanish and Portuguese were regularly used as galley slaves in ships crossing the Atlantic. Once in the New World, these Muslim slaves were assigned to labor on sugar plantations and in the mining operations of, among other places, Cuba and Brazil.

In 1586, Sir Francis Drake, commanding 30 English ships, made a daring raid against his Spanish and Portuguese enemies on the coast of Brazil. During this raid, Drake liberated some 400 Portuguese- and Spanish-held prisoners, including an estimated 300 Moorish and Turkish galley slaves as well as several dozen South American Indians, a smaller number of West African Muslims and a few Portuguese soldiers. Drake had planned to arm and release Turks and Africans on Cuba, to serve against the

THE ENIGMATIC OLMEC HEADS

Huge sculptures of heads with no bodies were made by the Olmec people, the first technically advanced Mexican people of whom we have knowledge. Their culture appeared in the coastal area of La Venta, a pre-Columbian archaeological site located in the present-day Mexican state of Tabasco, and they built earthen pyramids of considerable size not long after 1100 B.C. Their tombs were found to contain small toys with wheels, the first and only demonstration that any natives of the New World had knowledge of the wheel. But the Olmecs apparently never applied the technology for any functional use. The culture mysteriously ended about 400 B.C., perhaps by migration elsewhere or by enemy destruction. The gigantic stone heads are apparently all male and wear a stylized headdress reminiscent of the headgear of the Nubian Guard of the pharaohs. The ancient Africans, however, never even made it to the island of Madagascar. If these stone sculptures were based on the faces of Negroes encountered by Olmec artisans, the subjects would have to have been brought to Central America by one of the major seafaring cultures of the Old World.

Spanish, but heavy storms forced him to continue up the coast of North Carolina.

There, on Roanoke Island, he was besieged by English settlers pleading for a ride home to England. The English colonists had had enough of the New World. To fulfill their wish, Drake had to make room for them on his already crowded ships. According to English records, only 100 Turks were taken back to England, where they were ransomed to the Turkish Dominions. There is no further mention of the remaining 200 Moors, Turks, West Africans, Portuguese soldiers or the South American Indians liberated by Drake, and records show that Sir Walter Raleigh, who visited the island two weeks later, found no trace of them. Where did they go?

Research indicates that Drake left them behind, assuring them that he or someone would be back for them. But that was no guarantee of safety from the pursuing Spanish and Portuguese. On Roanoke Island they were little more than sitting ducks. There is little doubt they made their way the short distance to the mainland, probably utilizing the small boats left behind by the English, and then traveled steadily inland.

Within the next decade or so they encountered the remnant of the Santa Elena colony, many of whom shared their Muslim heritage. And there, thousands of miles from their homelands, these two surviving groups became one people.

In 1654, the English explorers learned from Southeastern Indians of a colony of bearded people wearing European clothing, living in cabins, smelting silver and dropping to their knees to pray five times daily (an Islamic custom), wherever they might be—a people who did not speak English but "Portyghee." In the mid-1600s there were people living among the Powhatans and related tribes of Virginia and North Carolina who were described as dark (like Indians) but called "Portugals." A similar people in

South Carolina called themselves Turks.

In the 1690s, French explorers reported finding "Christianized Moors" in the Carolina mountains. When the first English arrived in the mid-1700s, large colonies of so-called "Melungeons" were already well established in the Tennessee and Carolina Mountains. And in broken Elizabethan English they called themselves "Portyghee," or by the more mysterious term "Melungeon."

Over the years, as growing numbers of Scotch-Irish settlers swept upon them, Melungeons were pushed higher and higher into the mountains, and their claims of Portuguese heritage were increasingly ridiculed. Even the word "Melungeon" became a most disparaging term. In fact, to be legally classified as a Melungeon meant, in the words of one journalist, to be "nobody at all."

The Melungeons, pushed off their lands, denied their rights and mistreated, became an embittered and nearly defeated people. Over the ensuing decades, in a vain effort to fit in with their Anglo neighbors, they lost their heritage, their culture, their names and their original religion but not their genetic structure.

Perhaps the most stunning evidence is the gene frequency research conducted in 1990 by Dr. James Guthrie, who performed a reanalysis of 177 Melungeon blood samples taken in 1969, in east Tennessee and southwest Virginia.

Dr. Guthrie compared the frequency of certain genes within the Melungeon sample to the known genetic makeup of nearly 200 other world population groups. His findings indicated no significant differences between the Melungeon people of east Tennessee and SW Virginia, and the people of north Africa and especially Morocco, Algeria and Libya and the Galician mountains of Spain and Portugal, Iraq, Cyprus, Malta, the Canary Islands and extreme southern Italy, and most interestingly certain South American Indians, and, last but not least, the Turks.

Can it be pure coincidence that these gene frequency comparisons match up so perfectly with those populations theorized to be the source of the Melungeons? Can this sort of coincidence truly exist? There are also a number of medical conditions associated with the Melungeon people, e.g. sarcoidosis, a debilitating and sometimes fatal disease which is primarily a disease of Arabic, north African and Portuguese people with links to the Canary Islands. In this country it is most common among Caucasian Americans of Melungeon descent and African-Americans with Southeastern roots. Both groups undoubtedly derive in part from the same Mediterranean and Middle Eastern gene pool.

There is strong evidence that Christopher Columbus himself suffered from sarcoidosis. And there are other genetically related illnesses as well. Familial Mediterranean Fever, thallasemia and Machado Joseph Disease (also known as Azorean Disease) are all strong indicators that Melungeons are indeed of mixed Mediterranean, Middle Eastern, and north African and west African descent.

What can the long-standing mystery word "Melungeon" possibly mean? It was used by Spanish and Portuguese Berbers to describe themselves. But now there is yet another hint, further substantiating a Muslim origin. There are two Turkish words; "*melun*" meaning "cursed" or "damned" and "*can*" meaning "life" or "soul." Used together these words translate "one whose life or soul has been cursed," which would seem quite appropriate for 200 Muslim Turks an ocean away from their loved ones and their country.

The Melungeons, victims of an early form of ethnic cleansing, are the ancestors of a significant number of present-day Americans—Americans who may not know they are descended from Muslims, Arabs, Berbers, Africans and Indians, Portuguese and Spanish. The Melungeons, though most today are Christian, are the living legacy of Islam's first waves of immigration to the New World.   ❖

REFERENCE:

The Melungeons: The Resurrection of a Proud People, by N. Brent Kennedy with R.V. Kennedy, Mercer University Press, First Edition, 1994 (also, revised Fourth Edition 1997).

BIBLIOGRAPHY

Ball, Bonny Sage, *Melungeons: Their Origin and Kin*, Virginia Book Co., Berryville, Virginia, 1977.

Bible, Jean Patterson, *Melungeons: Yesterday and Today*, Continuity Press, Blountville, Tennessee, 1975.

Demarce, Virginia Easley, *Tennessee's Melungeons and Related Groups*, audiotapes.com.

Elder, Pat Spurlock, *Melungeons: Examining an Appalachian Legend*, Continuity Press, Blountville, Tennessee, 1999.

Kennedy, N. Brent, with Robyn Vaughn Kennedy, *Melungeons: The Resurrection of a Proud People*, Mercer University Press, Macon, Georgia, 1997.

Kennedy, N. Brent, *Unlocking Melungeons' Ancestry: The Making of a Documentary*, audiotapes.com.

Nassau (formerly McGlothlen), Mike, *Melungeons and Other Mestee Groups*, self-published, 1994.

Above, ancient "tower beacons" or cairns overlook the village of Cupids on Conception Bay in Newfoundland. It is certain that they were not built by Eskimos, who build cairns in a different and cruder style. Their origin is unknown, but it is considered likely by some researchers that they were erected by pre-Viking whites from Europe or Vikings themselves. The biggest of the known cairns is 14 feet tall. Right, a closeup of the tower beacon above.

DID AN UNKNOWN 'PRE-VIKING' CULTURE ROAM CANADA?

BY JOHN TIFFANY

L ittle is known about the people called the Picts, who preceded the Kelts in occupying the British Isles. Even less is known about the people who lived there before the Picts. We do not know what they called themselves, nor what language they may have spoken, as they were pre-literate. Farley Mowat has called these people "Albans." According to the Canadian author, the Albans traveled widely, even coming to the Americas, long before the rise of the Vikings.

In ancient times, Britain bore the name of Alba (hence the reference to modern England as "perfidious Albion"). But she was far from being alone in doing so. In fact, tens of scores of places with names derived from the root "alb" (possibly meaning "white") are, or were, to be found, scattered all over the map from Afghanistan to the Atlantic Ocean. More than 300 such place names have survived to the present —and many more are to be found in Asia Minor and northern Africa. The Alpine massif was originally called Albin. We may note also the Albania Superior and Albania Inferior in the Caucasus and Armenia, the Albania of the Balkans, Alba Longa in Italy, Alba and Albicet in Spain. The old name of the Tiber River (which was renamed by the Indo-European Romans) was Albula, home to a water nymph named Albunea. In the seventh century B.C., Britain was home to a society making the transition from bronze age to iron age. We do not know what they called their homeland, but the Carthaginian and Greek visitors called it Alba.

Farley Mowat, in his book *The Farfarers: Before the Norse* (1998, Steerforth Press, South Royalton, Vermont), concludes the name was closely associated with, if not the generic name of, the majority of the "indigenes" who inhabited Europe, Asia Minor and probably also northern Africa, until they were displaced, at least from their lowland territories, by various invading tribes, mostly of the Indo-European group, who burst into Europe from the east and southeast about 1500 B.C. and comprise the overwhelming majority of modern Europeans.

A likely example of a surviving group of Albans, Mowat says, is in the tiny ethnic group called Albkhazastanis, found on Mount Elbrus (pronounced by locals as "Albrus") in the Georgian part of the Caucasus. They do not speak Georgian or Russian but a tongue of their own.

The Albans produced a number of seafaring offshoots. Among them were, according to Mowat, the Basques, Aquitanians and Armoricans of northwestern Spain and the Bay of Biscay, and the Alpuani of the southwestern Italian Alps and Liguria, who sailed to and settled the islands of Corsica, Sardinia and Elba (Alba).

The much-feared Kelts, a group of headhunting slavers, began invading Britain by the fourth century B.C. Ireland was also invaded by about the third century B.C., and in due course most of Erin was occupied by the warlike Kelts, who displaced the presumably "Alban" peoples known in Irish mythology as the Tuatha

De Danaan and the Firbolgs.

Meanwhile, in Great Britain, it took until as late as the first century B.C. for the Kelts to overrun the difficult terrain of Cornwall (they were also hindered, it appears, by the Armorican allies of the Cornish native people); and their northward advance was slowed by the mountains and highlands. The autochthonous peoples of Wales, Cumbria and the Pennines held out for centuries. By about the middle of the second century B.C., the Keltic invasion had dragged to a halt somewhat to the south of the Cheviot Hills, in what today would be called southern Scotland, although later developments would lead to nearly all of Scotland being taken over by the Kelts.

However, a new and ruthless power was rising in the area—imperial Rome. By 51 B.C., the Armoricans were defeated by the Romans, and thousands of them, armed and unarmed, were slaughtered. The survivors—among them the Picts, Mowat thinks—may have fled to Scotland, where the native Albans may have allowed them to settle in the south of their country, to form a buffer against the Kelts to the south.

However, the Mowat theory seems to be based upon his identification of an Armorican tribe called the Pictones with the Picts of Scotland and Ireland. The counter to this argument is the fact that the term "Pict" was applied to them by the Romans, because the ancient Caledonians were in the habit of putting "pictures" on their skins, perhaps by tattooing. Thus the word "Pict" is derived from the Latin *pict*, the stem of pingere, "to paint," denoting anything pictorial, such as in "pictogram."

Mowat argues that the "Albans" of northern Scotland, who traded in walrus tusk ivory, called *valuta*, sailed west to Iceland, which was called Tilli, and to Greenland, which was known as Crona. (Greenland is, of course, part of North America.) They also sailed farther west, exploring and settling in Canada, around the Baffin Basin and into the Kane Basin, and probing into Hudson Strait and Ungava Bay, traveling through the peninsula of Ungava and exploring Hudson Bay. They also penetrated along the coast of Labrador and into Newfoundland (Alba-in-the-West) and the mouth of the St. Lawrence Seaway.

Writes Gunnar Thompson in his *American Discovery* (Misty Isles Press, Seattle, 1994):

> **The Arab geographer al-Idrisi wrote in his *Nuzhet al-Mustaq* (A.D. 1154) about the rich fishing in the North Atlantic (the Grand Banks of Newfoundland) and described the whalebone huts of Labrador's Eskimo natives. He also reported mariners' tales of natives living on "Saun," an island across the western ocean. According to Arabic mariners, the natives of Saun were naked except for a covering of leaves. The men were beardless and had the breath of "wood smoke." Some scholars believe al-Idrisi's account is evidence of an actual visit [by Muslims] to the Americas, where the natives smoked tobacco. The geographer also mentioned "Albania," or "Great Ireland," which he identified as a territory beyond Greenland. Apparently, the Arabs were aware of Keltic-Irish settlements in North America.**

The Romans withdrew from the British Isles, and the western Roman empire had its fall around A.D. 500. By 550-600, Pictland was beleaguered on the south and west. The northern islands were being raided by the Irish and the Saxons. The Picts and the Albans joined forces, and the old kingdom of Alba in Scotland was reborn. However, a new threat was to arise: the fury of the Northmen. Around 650-700, the Norse acquired their first truly seaworthy vessels and began venturing westward, reaching Shetland and Orkney, as peaceful traders initially, but relations soon turned to raiding.

In 729, Oengus, king of Scottish Alba, tried to recover Shetland and Orkney, but his fleet was destroyed. The Norse overwhelmed the islands, and the inhabitants fled west to Tilli, where crofts had been established previously. The Vikings, however, eventually followed. About 850, a Viking with the seemingly un-Viking-like name of Naddod sailed to Iceland, probably on a raiding venture. He was only the first of many, who were to make Iceland a part of Scandinavia. The majority of *valuta* clans seem to have emigrated to Crona before Viking raids on Tilli became a major threat.

For half a century, Alban settlements flourished in peace in Greenland, while the Vikings fought among themselves in Iceland. The first Viking settler in Greenland was, of course, Erik the Red (A.D. 985). Erik called his settlement Brattahlid.

By this time, according to most authorities, the Picts and/or Albans of Scotland and Ireland had been assimilated by the Gaelic Kelts. Since these people were nearly all Christian by the era of the Vikings, it is a moot point to say whether they were "Albans" or simply Scottish and Irish Christians. Here we will adopt Mowat's approach of referring to them as "Albans." In many cases, they were unable to effectively fight the Vikings, and chose to flee instead. (It is well known that Irish Christians, particularly Irish monks, were frequently targeted by the Vikings, and thus many of them headed for friendlier shores.)

With the arrival of the Norse pirates, most Cronian "Albans" were grimly aware of what such raids presaged for the future, as had happened before in the northern isles and then in Tilli, and therefore they departed for the American lands to the west.

After some five centuries of human habitation, Brattahlid lay abandoned for another five, during which time its stone and turf walls and sod roofs subsided into shapeless mounds. These were excavated in the 1930s by Danish archeologists. The spades revealed that during the centuries of Norse occupancy, a number of rooms had been added to and around an original single-roomed structure.

This structure is of special interest. Referred to in the archeological literature as the "earliest house known from Greenland," its walls enclosed a space about 50 feet long by 15 wide, corresponding in size and shape to the structures in the Canadian Arctic identified by Mowat as boat-roofed houses. However, the turf and stone walls of this building were as much as 12 feet thick—far thicker than needed for roof support or insulation. Mowat suspected that these massive walls were designed as much to defend the inhabitants against aggression as to provide shelter from the weather. Mowat elaborates:

> **The impression that the house was intended to double as a bastion capable of withstanding siege is reinforced by the presence within the walls of a stone channel bringing water from a concealed external spring. Excavation of three other very early Greenlandic houses has revealed similar built-in water supplies, together with exceptionally thick walls. Notably, such features have not been reported from houses of indisputably Norse origin in either Greenland or Iceland. I conclude that the original house on the Brattahlid site was probably built by Alban refugees from the Norse invasion of Tilli.**

If the structure was intended as a defense against the Norse polytheists, obviously it failed, in the end.

By 900, Alban walrus hunters appear to have rounded southern Greenland, gone north to the head of Baffin Bay, and reached Hudson Bay and Ungava Bay to the westward.

In the 1960s, Mowat visited the Oblate Mission at Povungnituk in Ungava, where the priest in charge, Father Steinman, told him of the 1948 crossing of the peninsula from west to east by Jacques Rousseau, chief archeologist of Canada's National Museum, accompanied by young French anthropologist Jean Michéa. Steinman remarked that the route had not previously been traveled by white men—"not in our time, anyway." But, as he told Mowat:

The Inuit [Eskimos] say it's a well-marked road. Many cairns along the way. Big ones—not *inuksuak* [Eskimo-style cairns]. The old people say they were built by Kablunait—white men—before the Inuit came into the country. I can show you a picture of one on the coast not far from here. It used to have a twin, but a couple of years ago prospectors pulled it down to see if there was a message in it. [Evidently there was no such hidden message.—Ed.]

The remaining "twin" stood (and perhaps still does) on Cape Anderson, the northern point of Povungnituk Bay. It is a massive cylinder, about 10 feet tall and more than four in diameter. It is artfully laid up of flat stones, some of them weighing an estimated 300-400 pounds. Steinman told Mowat there were more like it in the island labyrinth at the mouth of the Kogaluk River.

In 1957, Rousseau sent a new employee, William Taylor, north to investigate the sites. Taylor flew to Payne Lake, where he made some findings that smelt of a European presence. Although usually meticulous about reporting on his fieldwork, Taylor never did publish a full account of his dig at Payne Lake. Many years later, Mowat asked him why, and Taylor replied forthrightly that any suggestion of a European component in a pre-Columbian Arctic site would have "given the high priests of the profession conniptions. . . . I was a new boy in the field, so who was I to rock the boat?"

Taylor also visited Pamiok Island at the mouth of the Payne estuary. There he was shown what he described as an immense, stone-built foundation unlike anything previously reported from the North American arctic. He turned a few sods but left the island the same day. He never did return to excavate this extraordinary anomaly. But the ambivalence of his attitude toward it showed in the Eskimo name he gave the site—Imaha—which translates as "maybe." Taylor was unwilling to "slam the door" on the possibility of ancient Europeans in North America, but on the other hand he was unwilling to risk his career on such a notion. In any case, he assumed that if these were Europeans, they must have been Norsemen. The idea of pre-Viking visitors to these shores, not surprisingly, seems never to have occurred to him.

In the year 1025, Icelander Gudleif Gudlaugson landed in Newfoundland, where he encountered people possessing horses. These could not have been "Skraelings," as the Vikings called Indians and Eskimos, because these peoples apparently did not have the use of the horse until after the Spanish landed in America. The mention of horses in the sagas has been used by a number of historians to discredit the whole story, because they assume that there were no white people in America prior to the Vikings. But the Albans had horses, and undoubtedly took them along on their peregrinations.

The years 1380 to 1400 mark the period of the Zeno voyages to Labrador, Newfoundland and Nova Scotia, and at this time, people were still to be found there who constituted a society recognizable to a European as one cut from much the same cloth as his own.

A mysterious race of people still persists in Newfoundland who probably trace their ancestry back, in part, to the "Albans," specifically of the Basque strain. These people are known as Jakatars and are said to look rather like gypsies. The word "Jakatar" (which is spelt in various ways, including Jack-a-tar, Jakotar, Jackitar, Jockataw and Jacqueetar) first appears in the historical record as an entry in a journal kept by the Anglican minister at Sandy Point, St. George's Bay. On May 23, 1857, Rev. Henry Lind wrote: "Went to see a poor man. . . . He and all his family belong to a much-despised and neglected race called Jack a Tars. They speak an impure dialect of French and Indian, [are] R.C.s [Roman Catholics] and of almost lawless habits."

In the middle ages, a Basque word for God was *Jakue*, a variant on *Jainko* (hence the English expression, "By Jingo!"). *Tar* is a Basque suffix signifying a connection with, so *Jakue Tar* in 15th-century usage could have been an acceptable way to describe a Christian. Whatever their origin and the origin of their name, Jakatars consider themselves a people in their own right and declare southwestern Newfoundland, especially St. George's and Port au Port bays, to be their native and ancestral land.

Reconstructing ancient cultures by looking at potsherds and other artifacts is comparable to trying to deduce the plot of a stage play by examining the props. It is a challenge that calls for a lot of imagination. Farley Mowat, a professional storyteller, is well suited to the job. However, he has failed to provide convincing evidence for his theory that a single ethnic group, which could be called, as he does call them, "Albans," once existed throughout most of Europe before the Indo-Europeans. Nevertheless, his book does present significant, suppressed evidence of the presence of white explorers and traders in Canada before the Vikings.

Russell Burrows, a colonel in the reactivated state militia of Illinois, emerges from a cave which, he claims, he used as a "decoy" cave to deceive those who were constantly following him to learn the location of the cave that now bears his name. He also says that the "real" cave contains burial crypts, armor and thousands of ancient Old World-style artifacts.

THE BURROWS CAVE ENIGMA

BY JOHN TIFFANY WITH FRED RYDHOLM

A spelunker named Russell Burrows from the southern Illinois town of Olney allegedly discovered a mysterious cave along a branch of the Little Wabash River. If even some of the stories told surrounding this mysterious event are true, what are said by some to be the startling contents of the cave would set traditional American archeology on its ear.

In 1982, Russell Burrows was a man with a hobby: He liked to explore places that had been untouched for a long time. He knew of one region in Illinois where, according to rumor, there had once been a number of old homesteads. Burrows decided to explore the area. Burrows headed into the rugged, wooded countryside. He carried a metal detector, with which he hoped to locate relics of a century and more past: parts of old stoves, lamps, wedges, ax heads and other traces of early settlers and homesteaders.

Burrows stopped to eat his lunch on a bluff that overlooks a valley. He stood up and stepped on the edge of a flat, round rock. His weight on the side of this rock flipped it as if on a pivot, and

Burrows found himself falling into a pit below the rock. What happened next is told in his own words:

> **I found myself falling into a pit which had been secreted beneath a large oval stone which, as I later discovered, was fitted into the pit opening and designed to flip or turn over when stepped on. The unfortunate victim would fall to the bottom of the pit, the stone would swing back in place and the victim would be trapped. I was fortunate: When I stepped on that stone, I was in the act of turning, and the stone, instead of flipping over, slid off to one side and left the pit open.**
>
> **I do not actually remember hitting bottom; my next recollection is of hanging on to the lip of the pit by my elbows, in great alarm. I admit that I have a great fear of holes that I'm not ready for, because of snakes. But I found none. When I freed myself and regained my composure, I began to examine the pit and have a look at what was to be the beginning of the greatest adventure of my life. . . . I sat down to calm my nerves, catch my breath and give the situation some thought.**

Burrows found himself in a chamber, with a huge face on one of the walls.

> **I did not have to be a genius to figure out that I had stumbled into something that just should not be in Illinois. I have hunted for and found many artifacts of the American Indians, and there are many of their sites in my part of the state, but I knew then that this was not American**

Indian. The face I had been nose to nose with was different from anything I had ever seen. The nose was flat, the eyes were wide set, and the lips were thick.

Then, of course, there were all those strange symbols to consider. I had crawled under a ledge and was looking for petroglyphs such as I had seen in the pit. I had searched all the walls of the entire length of the valley, and while I had seen a few scratchings, I was not all that excited about what I had seen so far. Finally, I gave up on this last place, and decided to quit. In disgust, I tossed my small rock pick against the inside wall of the overhang. The rock gave out a distinctly unnatural sound: a hollow ring, not what I'd expect from solid rock. . . . As it was now clear that a cave was on the other side. . . . My first entrance was through this portal and into a tunnel-like passage which has a drop-off of about three feet just inside of the portal. I was met with a strong, musty odor. Not of decay, but musty.

As I moved my head and light around, I saw a full human skeleton reposing on a large block of stone. It scared the hell out of me! Then I began to see other things lying there with those bones. I saw ax heads, spear points, and something else—metal! The skeleton was laid out upon a solid block large enough to hold not only the remains but artifacts as well. The artifacts include ax heads of marble and other stone material, an ax head of what appears to be bronze, a short sword of what appears to be bronze, and other artifacts which might be considered personal

weapons. There were also a set of three bronze spears, the longest being about six feet long and the shortest about three feet. . . . The skeletal remains bear several fine artifacts such as armbands, headbands and other such items, all of gold.

The cave is said to lie somewhere along the Skillet Fork of the Little Wabash River in southeastern Illinois. It supposedly contains 13 elaborately ornamented burial crypts. It is unclear and a matter of controversy who, besides Burrows, has actually been inside the cave.

But Burrows has produced hundreds, if not thousands, of curiously carved stones that he says came from the cave. And some of the artifacts allegedly were not of stone, but of gold. It is claimed that Burrows sold off enough artifacts to unknown buyers that he was able to place $7 million in Swiss numbered bank accounts. According to Swiss journalist Luc Buergin, this money derives from the illegal sale of gold artifacts from the North American burial site. (Other sources claim that Burrows melted down all the gold and sold it as ingots. Still others question whether there ever was any gold in the first place.)

Buergin accuses Burrows of having clandestinely sold thousands of "burial gifts." In his recently published book *Geheimakte Archeologie* ("Secret file: Archeology," ISBN 3-7766-7002-9, Munich 1998) he presents documents, financial papers and pictures which indicate that Burrows has removed enormous quantities of gold from the cave system.

TBR managed to reach Mr. Burrows personally at his home in Windsor, Colorado on August 15. He told us that Buergin got his information from Harry Hubbard and Rick Flavin, "both of whom are high school dropouts. Hubbard is trying to sell stock in a company called Ptolemy Productions, but has been on the run from the police for selling fraudulent stock for over a year. Flavin is a guy who stole artifacts from a woman in Cadillac, Michigan and who just likes to shoot his mouth off."

Fred Rydholm is an amateur archeologist (with 50 years' experience) who, along with Russell Burrows, authored a book about the site, called *Mystery Cave of Many Faces*. TBR interviewed him regarding the discovery, which many have labeled a hoax. Rydholm was asked how much gold, in terms of weight, has been taken out of, or is in, Burrows Cave. He replied that Burrows claims "huge amounts" of gold are involved. However, Rydholm himself has only seen one small box of golden artifacts, and has not examined them closely. Burrows himself told TBR that over a ton of gold was found in the cave, and that none of it ever left.

According to Hu McCulloch of the Economics Department at Ohio State University, Vol. 3, No. 16 of *Ancient American* magazine "has a series of interesting articles on the Burrows Cave, which is surely either the biggest find or biggest running hoax of 20th-century American archeology."

McCulloch said on the Internet: "Most if not all of the 'gold' on the cover and inside *Ancient American* is known to be gold-painted lead casts of purported original artifacts." (He did not explain how this was known.)

TBR asked Rydholm, "Has any of the gold been analyzed to determine its origin or fineness?" "I don't know anything about that," he replied. Burrows told TBR that none of it was ever tested. However, he was of the belief that the gold must be very fine, "because you can bend it with a thumbnail."

Rydholm was asked whether any accepted or establishment organization has taken an interest in Burrows Cave. And if so, what have they done?

He replied that a Dr. John White, of Columbus, Ohio, who is a physicist and is also an officer in the Midwestern Epigraphic Society, believes the artifacts are authentic. Zena Halpern, of the

THOUSANDS OF ARTIFACTS EMERGE FROM BURROWS CAVE

HERE ARE REPRODUCED photographs of just a few of the thousands of stone artifacts that have been removed from the Burrows Cave archeological site. Skeptics point to the naive style of the carvings to prove that the finds could not have been made by Old World craftsmen. But no one can know for sure the historical scenario. Did the original Old World craftsmen die in the New World? Did ancient amateur craftsmen attempt to reproduce the work of professionals and fall short? Did American Indians carve the stones based on the works of Old World professionals, or under the supervision of these visitors? Did the Indians worship these Old Worlders, or did they have a hostile relationship with the arrivals? Or are the artifacts fakes—plain and simple? We may never know.

1. A crouching lioness. 2. A portrait of a man in what appears to be an Egyptian headdress and a sun symbol. 3. What looks like an American Indian with a mohawk, feathers and ornaments. 4. A reclining jackal. 5. An odd square-jawed portrait head with a helmet/headdress. 6. A stylized male lion.

Midwestern Epigraphic Society and the Institute for the Study of American Culture (ISAC), is working on an inscription that she claims appears to portray a Jewish menorah, from the cave. He said she also claims that a silver menorah was removed from the cave by Burrows.

White said:

> **I have not been confronted by physical evidence that would tend to prove it is a fraud. I am a scientist, and the type of things that have been said that are negative seem to have little substance; but they do open your eyes to the possibility that you are never really sure, even when you enter a major museum. Very few artifacts have a good pedigree. No more than 1-10 percent really have a good pedigree. Nearly always (in museums, for example) they are called Greek because they look Greek; they are called Egyptian because they look Egyptian.**
>
> **By the way, I have no certainty that there is a Burrows Cave. I am just talking about the artifacts. So you look at these artifacts, and they look old. I know nothing about the gold objects, other than just the talk. As long ago as 1994, I was offered a chance to pick up a set of lead replicas. I have about 50 replicas that are gold painted. I am sort of an authority on Burrows' propaganda. If it is fraudulent, it would have taken a team of about 10 experts and I do not know how many craftsmen to make them. The going price for these objects would not compensate anyone for making them. No one that I have ever been introduced to has ever seen the cave, other than Burrows.**

"What I can authenticate," Zena Halpern told TBR, "is a very, very rare menorah with a triangle base.

The unusual aspect of a triangle base menorah is what distinguishes these stones and makes them so unique. There are only two known examples in ancient Jewish sources of this unusual menorah with a triangle base, and they date from the first century B.C., when the menorah still stood in the Second Temple. Prior to the destruction of the Second Temple, menorahs were not depicted due to the prohibition against reproducing sacred objects from the temple. However, after the destruction of the temple in 70 A.D., in about the second and early third centuries A.D., menorahs began to be represented in the diaspora, and they all had three legs as a base. The first example of a menorah with a rare triangle base is relatively unknown and is found on coins minted by the last Judean king in the years from 40 to 37 B.C. The name of the king appears on the coins: Mattathias Antigonus II. This was a daring and innovative act for the king, as the reproduction of the menorah was forbidden by Jewish law. However, he was engaged in a desperate struggle against Herod and the Roman legions for control of Jerusalem, and he minted the coins as a Jewish symbol to rally the people to his cause. This triangle-base menorah never appeared again on coins and did not appear on any Jewish objects until the late second or early third centuries A.D., and when it appeared it had a base of three legs. The second example of a menorah with a triangle base is from an archeological dig in 1969 beneath

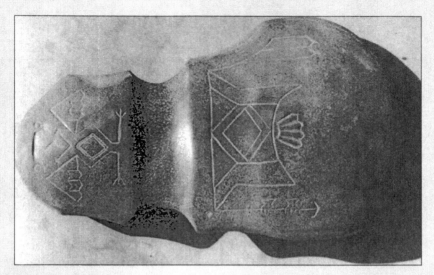

Here are two of the many finely crafted tools cave finder Russell Bur-
rows says were brought from the caverns. Above is a well-worked ax
head with a bird design and other ornamentation. Below is a spear
point, also finely crafted, with a decorative geometric motif. Were the
artifacts left by an as-yet-to-be-identified cult influenced by Old World
visitors to ancient Illinois? Or are they the work of an overly zealous
forger? If it was a forger, he must have worked night and day for
decades to create the volume of impressive artifacts removed and dis-
played from the underground crypts.

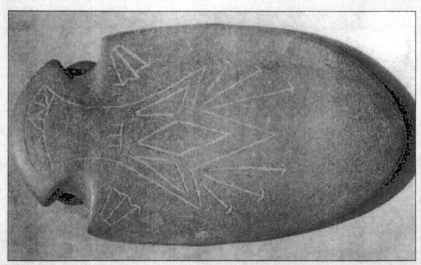

the Old City of Jerusalem from a house partially destroyed in the Roman assault on Jerusalem. This menorah was incised in plaster on the wall of the house and is considered the earliest clear depiction of the menorah which stood in the temple. It is dated to the Herodian era, 37-4 B.C. Prof. Nahman Avigad, director of the excavation, stated that the menorah had been found only a few hundred yards from the Temple Mount, and the artist probably saw the temple menorah every day. The depiction is rare because of the holiness of the object. (*New York Times*, Dec. 3, 1969) Two other objects were also represented on the plaster and were reconstructed to be the altar and the shewbread table, objects which stood in the temple. The golden menorah was carried off to Rome by Titus, and a representation of the menorah was carved on the Arch of Titus; but it had an octagonal base. A description of the construction of the menorah is given in Exodus 25:31-37, and while the specifications are [otherwise] extremely detailed, no mention is made of the base.

The appearance of this menorah, an obscure and rare object, from a brief window of time, on these stones remains an intriguing mystery. Along with the menorah, three ancient Hebrew letters also appear on the stones, which are yod, heth and daled, possibly an ancient spelling of "Judea," but more analysis is needed to confirm this. There are also depictions of sacred objects from the temple on some of the stones such as the shewbread table, musical instruments and a possible shofar. There are many unresolved questions remaining about the cave, and much controversy has occurred over the years. However, the reproduction of this rare, triangle-base menorah poses a most intriguing and fascinating mystery.

Prof. Cyclone Covey, a historian who has studied many languages and epigraphy, is convinced the cave is genuine. He stated:

Carthaginian religion was Egyptian, and their outpost was the Siwa oasis, a place visited by Alexander the Great, and called by them Amonia, from the Egyptian god Amon. It was a famous oracle throughout antiquity because it was like the Delphic oracle; it was one of the four major ones that could predict the future. It was visited by the Emperor Hadrian. All the Libyans of north Africa adhered to the Egyptian religion. The cave is an Egyptian-style mausoleum. The tombs of the kings of Egypt are constructed in the same way as those in Burrows Cave. They are water-tight. Burrows had not been to the tombs in Egypt, but his description matches it completely. Many of the stones from the cave are written in Numidian, and some are in Libyan, while others are in Ptolomaic Greek. The Yuchi Indians used to live in a large area, among all the tribes that were Algonquin speaking. Their own language is of Scythian derivation. The Yuchi tradition is that they had a sacred mausoleum in that vicinity, which they sealed, about A.D. 800. Cahokia rose like a mushroom and became the dominant power in the region. Russell did not know anything about this tradition when he discovered the cave. The cave owner was known as "Neff," but his real name was a lengthy Italian one. Carthaginian gold coins were molded, and they have a horse head on one side. The Yuchi tradition is that there was gold in the cave, and an archive. The Yuchis in the time of De Soto lived in houses, not teepees, and were lighter skinned than other Indians.

I do not think Burrows has made a lot of money out of the cave. He lives rather simply on his military pension, like lower middle-class people. He has a motorcycle, and not a Cadillac.

"Is it possible that the artifacts were manufactured by a 19th-century cult, as some have alleged?" he was asked.

No, sir, I think it is utterly impossible. Utterly impossible. There are no signs that the cave was discovered before Burrows fell into it. No one knew enough to fake Numidian, Keltiberian and other languages which were not known until the 20th century. It is like the Paraiba inscription that recounts how a Phoenician expedition was carried to Brazil, and the language in the inscription is Phoenician, which is very close to Hebrew and had certain turns of phrases that were unknown at the time the Paraiba inscription was discovered.

Wayne May, publisher of *Ancient American*, told TBR:

By the finder, a lot of gold has been taken out of the cave. Testing tells us there is still more gold in the ground. Burrows melted the gold down and sold it. He looted the site. Burrows now claims the site [which we are preparing to excavate] is not his site. A little over 7,000 artifacts have come out of the cave, not counting the gold items. A lot of scientists have looked at the material, but they are being quiet until the location of the site is divulged. We have an archeologist on hand, and will have Ho-Chunk [Winnebagoes] from Black River Falls, Wisconsin on the site upon opening late September this year [2001].

Burrows told TBR that, as a retired prison guard, he is living on Social Security, and that he manages to support a middle-class lifestyle on this as his only source of money.

Beverly Mosley, former director of art at the Ohio Historical Society, and currently president of Midwestern Epigraphic Society, told TBR:

There is a lot of creativity in these artifacts. Some of it is what we call minimal art, like Eskimo art. We are talking thousands of artifacts, and they are all different. They could not possibly have been made all by one person. There is no way in hell that the average Joe Schmo can put together an ancient style of writing and make it readable. There are probably 10 different alphabets written on these stones. For someone to duplicate these things, they are going to have to know five or six alphabets, and know how to draw things correctly. Probably out of the stones I have seen, I have seen 500 with ancient script on them. There is a lot of Iberian writing, ogam and tifinagh writing.

(Tifinagh is a script of unknown origin, used by the Tuaregs in certain objects, like bracelets and rock inscriptions.)

Geologist Dr. Jim P. Scherz (author of *Rock Art Pieces from Burrows Cave*) has studied the stone artifacts. According to him, there is weathering on their surfaces that proves the stones are very old, quite possibly going back to the time of Christ, if not older than that. Certainly they are far older than the century or so that some establishmentarians have suggested as a maximum.

Of course, it is not unusual for discoverers of "politically incorrect" evidence to run into serious problems with the establishment. In his book, Burrows tells of his first unpleasant brush with academia:

> **I contacted [Eastern Illinois University] and inquired if they had an anthropologist on their staff. They did, and I was put in contact with him. A meeting was arranged, and I made the trip up to the university to meet with this young fellow, whom I will refer to as Mr. "Brown." . . . This probably could have happened at a number of universities across the country. . . .**
>
> **The first thing he asked me was, "Where is the cave?" I told him I didn't want to reveal the location of it at that time because of the fact that I had not yet worked out an agreement with the land owner, and, as a matter of fact, I had not met him, nor did I know who he was. Brown was a little put out with the fact that I was not going to spill the whole pot of beans to him, but he said that he doubted the artifacts were all that old. He told me he would attempt to find out what they were and that he would get back to me as soon as he could. I left the university and made the trip**

back to Olney. While doing so, I was doing a lot of thinking. Why didn't he think those artifacts were old? . . . The trip home took about an hour. I sat down at the kitchen table to ponder the situation. Just as I was getting into my second cup, the telephone rang. It was Brown. "Great news," he said, "I found out what your artifacts are. I called the state archeologist at Champaign, and after I described the artifacts to her, she said, 'Oh, I know what those things are. They were made by a cult in southern Illinois about 100 years ago, and they must have hid them in caves or buried them.' " "You mean she was able to make that determination from your description by telephone?" I asked, when I found my tongue. "Oh, sure," came back Brown. "She is a very sharp person and has studied the history of southern Illinois at length. She really knows what she's talking about." What do you do when you are backed into a corner like that? My first thought was to walk away and forget it. They must have had a very low opinion of my judgment. But now I had the same opinion of theirs.

In conclusion, it can only be stated that nothing can safely be concluded regarding Burrows Cave at this time. Hopefully, sometime within the next few months, there may be some official statement by a university or reputable archeologist, but for now, all anyone has to go on is hearsay. Rydholm says that seismographic tests are presently being conducted around the site to verify the existence of chambers.

If it turns out that Burrows Cave is for real, it could be the hard evidence diffusionists have been looking for for a generation. Not many publishers would be disappointed either. It would mean every schoolbook in America would have to be reprinted with the truth about the feats and abilities of our ancient ancestors. ❖

ABOUT FRED RYDHOLM: A history teacher, lecturer and the co-author of The Mystery Cave of Many Faces, *Fred has spent more than 50 years exploring ancient sites in the Americas and the Old World searching for evidence that ancient explorers made it to the New World before Columbus. He may be the world's foremost expert on the archeological phenomenon of dolmens—odd configurations of one large boulder (many times 25, 50 or more tons) set upon three smaller boulders and sometimes located at the top of mountains. Establishment types want you to believe that these are glacial erratics but Fred is convinced they are the remains of tombs or altars left behind by some mystery culture of great antiquity. And he has thousands of slides and photographs to prove his point. Fred has always lived in the Upper Peninsula region of Michigan, where he also uncovered overwhelming evidence that the ancients mined copper in the Americas and shipped it back to the Old World, in effect providing the materials necessary to fuel the copper and bronze ages of old Europe. Fred enthralled the attendees at THE BARNES REVIEW'S SECOND INTERNATIONAL CONFERENCE ON AUTHENTIC HISTORY with his lectures and slide show on dolmens and ancient copper mining in Michigan. Fred is extremely proud to call himself an amateur archeologist, even though he has done more on-site research on these topics than any other man in the world. He is just the type of straight-shooting, commonsense scholar that makes bookish Ph.D.s and court historians nervous.*

A BURROWS CAVE SKEPTIC SPEAKS

BY STEPHEN LOMBARDO

Somewhere in southern Illinois, it is alleged, there is an amazing cave known as Burrows Cave, or, as some prefer to call it, Burrows Burrow. The reports are reminiscent of the tales of caverns filled with treasure in versions of **One Thousand and One Arabian Nights.** *Only the genie is missing, along with Aladdin's lamp. Is Burrows Cave real, or is it a hoax?*

The supposed owner of Burrows Cave, if it exists at all, is said to have allocated several million dollars for excavating the cave and to build a museum to house the findings. The fabulous cave is alleged to contain 13 tombs with human remains, a ton of gold and inscribed scrolls.

Among the people claimed to be entombed there is no less a personage than Alexander the Great. Scholars have been scouring the sands of Egypt for centuries looking for Alexander's final resting place, so Americans can take comfort in knowing that the followers of the mighty Macedonian ferried his Soma (as the body of Alexander is known) across the Atlantic and deposited it safely in a cave in the Midwest.

In an adventure worthy of Indiana Jones, Russell Burrows discovered the cavern named after him by stepping on a large stone covering a hole. If he had stepped on the inside half of the stone, he would have plunged to his death in a pit designed to trap intruders, as in the pharaonic tomb in the Valley of the Kings and some of the pyramids in South America.

Dr. Cyrus Gordon, professor emeritus of Brandeis University, is one of the world's top-rated linguists and Semitic scholars. Having heard of these Illinoisian legends, Gordon decided that if one-

10th of the tales were true, the cavern would indeed be a remarkable discovery. Gordon states:

I felt the coins [ancient gold coins alleged to have been taken out of the cave and depicted in a slide shown by Mr. Burrows], if genuine, were important enough to merit investigation rather than be brushed aside, *a priori*, as "too good to be true." (I remember when the caves that yielded the Dead Sea scrolls were considered "too good to be true.") However, until a trustworthy and competent scholar is permitted to examine the actual coins, we must countenance other scenarios such as that the slide could have been made from a recently contrived painting. No credible witness has, to my knowledge, seen the cave or the coins.

So Gordon arranged to examine the cave and some of the gold coins said to have been taken from it, under the guidance of Burrows. This was in June 1991, and the inspection was to take place October 19 and 20 of that same year.

After a month and a half had elapsed, Gordon received a couple of phone calls from Burrows, who warned the good doctor that a strenuous hike from the road to the cave was involved. Gordon assured Burrows that he was up to that—upon which Burrows added that the area was infested with snakes. Gordon informed the man that he had no great fear of poisonous reptiles, having had much experience with scorpions and other venomous varmints during his expeditions to the Near East. Gordon relates:

When his latter-day labors of Hercules failed to dissuade me, Mr. Burrows notified me (in a letter dated August 23, 1991) that the owner had re-

GOLDEN RICHES ALLEGEDLY FOUND IN MYSTERIOUS ILLINOIS CAVE

Some of the gold artifacts claimed to have been found in Burrows Cave. Clockwise from upper left: a medallion with an odd script; a "thunderbird" figure; what could be a "whale medallion"; a bearded "Phoenician-faced" medallion.

jected our long-planned visit to the cave site, for security reasons. However, Mr. Burrows courteously offered to show me some of the region in which the cave is allegedly situated and his collection of 115 artifacts from the cave. I declined this kind offer, because I have examined some of those finds and seen the photographs of many more. They are modern products, in which I am not interested. The "good stuff" (notably the gold) has been put back into the cave. . . . Maybe there is a tiny kernel of truth to the wild stories about Burrows Cave. But I have no time to search for it. I have other priorities.

(As of October/November, 1999, the count of mudstone artifacts alone has gone up to "an estimated 6,000-7,000 pieces.")

Burrows has since spread the word that Gordon was attempting to bully him out of the cave and take it over as his own, which this writer considers a dubious proposition.

In sum, we do not know who owns the cave, assuming there is a cave. But we do know it is not owned by Burrows. Does this mean that if Burrows is telling the truth, he is a trespasser and a thief? Furthermore, by removing artifacts without plotting their precise location etc. he is destroying priceless archeological information, if his tales are true. This goes against all the canons of modern scientific archeological methodology in which potsherds and their exact placement are fully as important as golden treasures. Alternatively, there may not be any cave, and Burrows may be nothing other than a hoaxer. In that case, he has defrauded a number of people to whom it would seem he has peddled his alleged "ancient artifacts." Either way, it does not look good for Burrows.

Certainly there is some serious evidence in existence (take, for example, some of the writings of Diodorus Siculus, a Greek historian who lived from 80 B.C. to 20 B.C.) that the ancient Phoenicians may have sailed to America. And King Juba II of Mauretania explored extensively throughout the Atlantic Ocean, to judge from what Pliny the Elder (Gaius Plinius, A.D. 23 to A.D. 79) wrote about him.

It is at least conceivable that the Greeks and Macedonians could have similarly crossed the sea. And it is possible that they might have taken Alexander's body to these shores. They might even have trekked inland to what is now Illinois and deposited his sacred remains there in a cave. Nothing would thrill this writer more than for such an astounding saga to be confirmed. But so far, unfortunately, despite plenty of opportunities and the passage of a considerable number of years, there has not emerged any real evidence that this happened.

The present writer does not hold himself out as an expert on ancient artifacts, but looking at pictures of the alleged objects, which are supposedly (and mysteriously) from several different classical cultures, one cannot but be struck by the sameness of their style, which is a clumsy and amateurish one. Thus one is naturally inclined to speculate that these items were actually manufactured in someone's garage or basement and not found in an ancient cave. However, we must withhold judgment for now. But until there is some credible evidence that emerges in this case, that can be studied by credible experts, we must agree with Dr. Gordon that we have no time for these matters, and that we have other, higher priorities. It would be a sad thing if Revisionists, who take pride in debunking longstanding myths, should fall for some other elaborate hoax.   ❖

BIBLIOGRAPHY:

Burrows, Russell E., and Rydholm, C. Fred, *The Mystery Cave of Many Faces*, Superior Heartland, Marquette, Mich., 1991.

"The 'Lost Tomb' of Alexander the Great and Other Problems," by Alexander P. McGregor Jr., in *Ancient American*, vol. 3, issue 21, Nov./Dec. 1997.

"The Greatest Discovery in the History of Archaeology: A New History for a New Century," by Horatio Rybnikar, in *Ancient American*, issue 16, 1996.

"An Ancient American Exclusive: Russell Burrows Speaks Out on the Mystery Cave," interview with Wayne May, in *Ancient American*, vol. 1, No. 4, Jan./Feb. 1994.

"Was the Voyage of Hanno's Story Told at Burrow's Cave Campfires?" by John J. White III and Beverly H. Moseley Jr., in *Ancient American*, vol. 1, issue 7, Sept./Oct. 1994

"Illinois State and Federal Laws and Burrows Cave," by Brig. Gen. (Ill. state militia) Russell E. Burrows, in *Ancient American*, issue 13, April/May 199.

Stephen Lombardo works for AMERICAN FREE PRESS, *a populist newspaper in Washington, D.C.*

Above, figures identified by researcher Robert F. Marx as sixth or seventh century A.D. Hindu deities uncovered in some ruins in Guatemala. Deep in the tropical forests of western Honduras at the ruins of Copan, there is a stone sculpture believed by some to be a representation of Indra, the chief deity of early Hindu religion, riding an elephant. The profile of two elephants appears on another stela (stone marker) at the same site. At Copan there are at least three images resembling Hanuman, the monkey-faced god celebrated in the Ramayana, one of India's greatest epics.

WHEN DID OUR ANCESTORS COME TO AMERICA?

BY RONALD P. ANJARD

Some historians have long thought that Christopher Columbus discovered America. Questions arose when a stone carving in Minnesota was attributed to an earlier Viking expedition. More recently, analyses of findings in North, South and Central America have raised substantial questions as to who really were our first visitors.

The famous Ra expedition of Thor Heyerdahl was intended to demonstrate that early crossing of the Atlantic was possible. There is extensive evidence that between 2000 B.C. and A.D. 200 these lands were visited not only by the Kelts, Egyptians, Libyans, Phoenicians, Iberians and Romans, but also Asians, including Japanese, Indians (from India) and Chinese.

This may sound preposterous. How can history be so wrong? Here is information integrated from many expert sources. This writer does not know of any other such compilation. The intent here is to present these data so that we all can truly better understand history. This writer proposes that we are now just scratching the surface of the truth of our ancient history.

Consider first the case of Central America—particularly the ancient Mexicans and the Mayans. There is much circumstantial evidence that the Mayans were directly influenced by major cultures in Europe, Asia and Africa. When this information is viewed as a whole, the information provided must be considered more than pure coincidence.

The Mayans, like the Babylonians of the same era (c. 500 B.C.), were accomplished mathematicians and astronomers. The Mayans were familiar with plane and spherical trigonometry, which enabled them to compute the size of the world, estimate the distance from pole to pole and calculate the length of a meridian. The Mayans knew how to add, subtract, multiply, divide and had a concept of zero. At that time in history, only the Mayans and Babylonians had the zero. The Mayans used a method of metrical calculation only redeveloped in the middle of the 19th century. Another important fact is that the Babylonians and Mayans were also the only civilizations able to handle the concept of millions.

The Mayan year was 365.2420 days. Our modern year is 365.2423 days. They likewise determined the length of the Moon's and Venus's cycle with very high accuracy. *The Dresden Codex* has been described as a highly sophisticated astronomical computer by the Institute of Mayan Studies of the Miami Museum of Science. *The Grolier Codex* is a calendar of the phases of Venus using a sophisticated system. *The Tro-Cortesianus Codex*, another astronomical computer, gives the synodic cycles of Venus, Mercury, Mars and Jupiter.

Consider now the Quetzalcoatl Pyramid in Teotihuacan, a Mayan site just north of modern Mexico City. By starting at its center as a mark for the Sun, and measuring along the precessional, Harleston found that all nine presently known planets plus another potential fell on definite markers, which were symmetrically spaced in what appeared to be a binary progression beginning with the number nine. Consider that it was not until late in the 18th century that more than the first five planets became known to modern man.

The "Aztec clock" is a cosmic clock of extreme sophistication. It showed an exact knowledge of cyclical movements of the planets, calculated their synodic returns equal to the accuracy of modern astronomers within five decimal points. This calendar enabled computation of solar and lunar eclipses, passages of the Sun at zenith, equinox and solstice, phases of the Moon, passage of Venus and even planetary conjunctions.

The star *Eta* of the constellation Draco virtually remained unchanged in right ascension from 1800 B.C. to A.D. 500. *Eta Draconis* provided the Mayans with an accurate measure of the sidereal years. The path of *Eta Draconis* correlated perfectly with the format in *The Madrid Codex*. The Mayans knew of 400 stars in the Seven Sisters constellation of the Pleiades, whereas only six or so stars can be seen with the naked eye.

Ancient Mexicans not only employed carefully oriented temples to determine equinoxes and solstices but even used ball courts, special details on buildings and others for astronomical observations. In codices, ancient astronomers are shown, as in Babylonia and Egypt, observing certain stars from a dark cell through openings in temples. The orientation of the Costillo at Chichén Itzá is so designed as to determine both the vernal and autumnal equinoxes. Many temples are aligned with other buildings for determination of equinoxes.

Stonehenge-like arrangements, similar in principle to those found in England, can be found near Copán, Mexico City and other Mesoamerican sites. Interestingly, near the Nazca River at Cahuachi, Peru, a "wood Stonehenge," a collection of wooden columns, has been dated as several millennia old. Dr. José Cabrera of the University of Peru has collected 14,000 stones with

BEARDED ANCIENT AMERICANS

Although American Indians today are generally unable to raise a real beard (unlike Caucasians), beards were by no means unknown in ancient America. The Mesoamerican sculpture on the facing page probably dates from about A.D. 700, before the rise of the Toltecs. Found in Tepatlzaco, it may represent the art of the "Nonoalcans," who formed part of the Toltec confederacy. The man at right of the relief is a nobleman about to take part in the sacred ball game. The man at left, evidently an important official himself, is fastening the first man's hip pad for the game. Players were forbidden to use their hands to hit the ball. Sometimes a player would be killed by the impact of the solid rubber ball, seven to eight inches in diameter. Note the wearing of protective knee pads, arm padding and protective bandages around the waist. Interestingly, both figures wear beards. This may represent a physical inheritance from Caucasoid voyagers from the Old World. Below, at the time of the collapse of the Mayan civilization we find new tribes appearing in the vicinity. Among these was the Putún, who either were white or else contained white elements among them. Here is a detail of Stela 11, Seibal, Guatemala. The non-Mayan features of this leader suggest that he may have been a Caucasoid Putún invader. Note the mustache, characteristic of the white race.

carved star maps, Peruvian Indians using telescopes and even extensive medical operations. These stone carvings have been dated by experts as being 3,000 years old.

The Mayan calendar starts at 3374 B.C. The many steles and elaborately carved buildings throughout Maya land are carefully dated, using hieroglyphs. This is evidence also of a very sophisticated culture and science.

The Cuicuilco Pyramid, lava covered, has been dated by accepted geological methods as being at least 7,000 years old. Studies have established a very advanced civilization. Consider also that there are three times as many pyramids in Central America as in Egypt. Both Mayans and Egyptians used step pyramids. The Mayans, also like the Egyptians, rarely used pyramids as tombs; pyramids were used for religious and astronomical purposes.

At the time of Rome, the Mayan city of Teotihuacan was the size of Rome and had north-south and east-west avenues with atrium-type apartment complexes. Teotihuacan has two major step pyramids: the Pyramid of the Sun and the Pyramid of the Moon.

A colossal head, at La Venta, Mexico, has a singularly Egyptian feature: a speaking tube that ran from a giant ear and emerged between two great stone lips. A stele also found near La Venta shows a figure with a pointed beard, an elaborate robe and headdress and even oddly turned-up shoes. Constance Irwin found that the Hittites and Phoenicians were the only ones in this period who wore long robes, turbans with ribbons, pointed beard and upturned shoes. This has been dated 500 B.C. by experts. Startling Semitic carved figures have been found in Mesoamerica with pointed hats, braided-like beards, pronounced noses, pointed shoes and even grapes hanging from their belts. In contrast, a stone lintel found at Lorrillard City shows a priest passing a rope through his tongue. The worshippers of Shiva, Hindu god of destruction, tortured themselves by drawing a rope through their own pierced tongues. Keep this in mind as you read further.

Throughout Maya land there is evidence of a phallic cult, similar to that of the Phoenicians. Wheeled terra-cotta toys are also found in Mesoamerica, which are similar to the terra-cotta toy chariots modeled by the Phoenicians.

During 15 years of investigation of thousands of terra-cotta pottery heads and figures, art historian A. Con Wuthenau found portraits of five different racial types: Mongol, Chinese, Japanese, Negroid and "all types" of white people—especially Semitic types, with and without beards.

A long-lasting puzzle still exists: Who made a perfectly fashioned crystal skull, 3,600 years old, found in the foothills of British Honduras (Belize today—Ed.)?

Mayan reliefs are strikingly similar to motifs in Buddhist countries. The Sun and serpent, two of the most sacred symbols of Buddhism, were also very important to the Mayans. The cult of the serpent existed from ancient times as far north as the mound builders of Indiana and Ohio. The serpent is still part of the Zuni and Hopi rituals. The Hopi, Aztec and Buddhist doctrine taught life after death and also that the world has been through four destructions already. Think about the earlier-mentioned "rope-through-the-tongue" concept also for a relationship to India.

A collection of steles and stones by Father Carlo Crespi of Ceunca, Ecuador, has been dated approximately 500 B.C. These tablet writings belong to the Brahmi class. Brahmi bears a considerable amount of similarity with some early north Semitic scripts. These are dated c. 1000 B.C. Brahmi originated in India. Continuing on this point, according to Dr. B. Ch. Chabra, on the famous Phallic Rock on Molokai, Hawaii, the inscription has been identified as being ancient Sanskrit. Like Hindus, the Mayans postulated rhythmic astronomical cycles. Gordon Eckholm, outstanding authority on ancient Mexico, has pointed out that some of the most significant parallels between Hindu-Buddhist and late-classic and post-classic Mayan art are those classified under the heading of lotus panels.

Quipus, or knotted cords, were used by Aztecs, pre-Incas, ancient Mexicans, Egyptians and even Chinese as mnemonic devices.

It was a custom among the Mayans, Egyptians, Chaldeans and Greeks for girls of royal blood to marry their brothers. Phoenicians were great child sacrificers, according to Hugh Fox. The whole sacrificial system was based on an attempt to prevent another and final great cataclysm. Historians have attributed similar motivations to the Aztec sacrificers.

Among the institutions and customs shared by the Phoenicians of the first millennium B.C. and the inhabitants of Central America in that era is an advanced knowledge of mathematics and astronomy. These were the only two ancient civilizations which had a place value in their mathematics, a concept of zero and the ability to express large numbers—1 million, for example. It was not until the 19th century that the concept of a million was common in the West.

Both civilizations had records of stars going back 370,000 years and estimated the period of the Moon to within a matter of seconds. While the Romans and other contemporaries thought the Morning Star and Evening Star were two different bodies, the Babylonians and Mayans knew them to be the same body, which we call Venus. Both used gnomons to measure the Sun's shadow and determine latitude. Other common features were pyramidal temples that rose in terraces and could be used for astronomical observatories as well as worship of the Sun, Moon and Venus; hieroglyphic writing, the custom of deforming heads of newborn

Above left, a photograph of the ancient Caucasoid race known as the Ainu in traditional garb. Note the heavy beard and broad facial features characteristic of his people. At right, two members of the Haida tribe of Northwest Coast Indians at a potlatch festival in 1900. The figure at left bears a striking resemblance to the Ainu with his heavy beard and broad face. The figure at right wears a smock with a motif reminiscent of Ainu textile patterns. Is there a connection?

children and use of incense.

An astonishing representation of the Mayan rain god, Tlaloc, is a figure of a white man with a handlebar mustache and long beard, holding a thunderbolt—just as did his Phoenician counterpart.

The *Chimal Book of Chilam Balam* [Chilam Balam is the Jaguar Prophet; his books are prophetic and quasi-historical. —Ed.] referred to the first inhabitants of that region, Yucatan, as coming from the east in boats. Another ancient writing said that a leader, Votan, returned several times to his former home across the Atlantic to the area referred to as Valum Chiuim. This locale has been identified by Mexican experts as Phoenicia.

Now consider the North American evidence. There are strange pieces of a puzzle in addition to the famous Minnesota Viking stone. At the Koster dig in western Illinois, archeologists from Northwestern University are now studying civilization at a depth of 8000 B.C. A University of Pittsburgh team has dated an excavation near Avella, Pennsylvania at 14,225 B.C. And in the San Diego area, civilization has been dated in excess of 30,000 B.C.

But there really is much more. In the past several years there have been major finds throughout the United States. These include sites, carvings and analyses of languages.

Mystery Hill at North Salem, New Hampshire, is truly an ancient American Stonehenge. Extensive studies have established it was both an astronomical and religious site. There are other similar sites in central Vermont and the foothills of the Green Mountains. The sites were used as gravestones, solar sightings and for various Keltic gods. Experts in epigraphy have identified the carvings as ogam, which is an old way of writing used by the Kelts. According to Barry Fell of Harvard, Kelts occupied Mystery Hill and related New England sites around 800 B.C., based on these important findings. In addition to numerous sites in New England, a few others have even been found in Oklahoma and Arkansas.

A very early penetration of New England was made by the Iberians. Rock carvings in Spain of seaworthy ships have been dated at 3500-2000 B.C. On Monhegan Island, 10 miles off the Maine coast, a settlement of ancient fishermen has been uncovered and related to the Iberians. Radiocarbon dates this location at c. 1800 B.C. At a Nova Scotia site, it has been estimated that the original construction may even have actually been around 3000-2000 B.C. These settlers may have been from Malta, based on analysis of very unusual carvings.

Further evidence of Mediterranean parallels in New England is scattered over all six states.

At Lake Assawompseh, Massachusetts, there is a carving of a ship very similar to a Minoan ship with high bow and stern and one square sail on a center mast. Near the White River, Vermont, there is a hieroglyphic inscription of the late Ptolemaic Egyptian era.

There is another riddle in Georgia. A wall near the summit of one of the highest mountains is greater than seven feet high and approximately 10 feet thick. It has been estimated as 2,000 years old by the Georgia Archaeological Department. Cherokee Indians have a legend that white men inhabited northern Georgia and Tennessee before the American Indians arrived.

Iberian magnetic compass dials were apparently copied by the Amerindians. A disk found in Tennessee is very similar to such dials from Liria, Spain. At Grave Creek and Braxton, West Virginia, tablets with Iberian inscriptions have been dated at c. 800 B.C.

Among the Algonquin materials at the Peabody Museum in Massachusetts is an old birch bark manuscript identified as of Cree (Ojibway) origin. Epigraphic analysis has determined that the script is actually of the ancient city of Palmyra, Spain. It was destroyed by the Romans in A.D. 272.

In 1885 an inscribed stone was discovered by the Smithsonian Institution in the excavation of a burial mound in Loudon County, Tennessee. Originally thought to be Cherokee, analysis now confirms the script to be ancient Hebrew, dated at c. A.D. 100.

On the Cimarron Cliffs, there are combined Libyan and Egyptian hieroglyphs. The Rio Grande Shishong Inscription has been identified as Libyan. In late 1976, *The Indianapolis Star* reported that Roman pottery had been found in Georgia and Alabama. Roman coins have been reported in a find near the Rio Grande in Texas.

The presence of Libyan inscriptions in the southwest and the occurrence of Libyan words in painted pottery of the Mibbers Valley, New Mexico, leads to the inference that the ancestors of the ancient Zunis composed one of the linguistic groups of ancient Maghrib Arabic, according to Dr. Fell.

There is an extraordinarily high incidence of ancient Arabic vocabulary in certain Indian languages. For example, the Zuni tribe, called *Shiwi* in their own tongue, speak what appears to be a creolized dialect of Libyan origin, probably related to the parent speech of the various north African tribes that called themselves by names similar to "Shiwi." The Zuni language is 50 percent Libyan.

In 1901, ancient Pima chants were collected during a Smithsonian expedition to Arizona. The almost total Arabic vocabulary of these chants also appears to be a creolized dialect derived from an Iberic or Arabic Maghrib province. The Pima language is rich in Punic (Carthaginian) words.

The Micmacs' language is 60 percent Egyptian. They still use hieratic script. The Wabanaki (Maine) language is 60 percent Phoenician and the rest Egyptian. Many of the New England names tend to be Keltic, especially the names of mountains and rivers.

Possibly the takeover of Europe by the "barbarians," the Muslim infiltration into Europe, the destruction of major libraries as in Alexandria and Rome, and the restrictions of the dark ages eliminated the records of the early visits to the Western Hemisphere.

Evidence shows that great sections of North America and Central America have been frequently visited by many ancient civilizations. These visits were extensive, approximately as early as

2000 B.C. and 500 B.C.

This material is presented not to discredit Columbus or even Leif Eriksson. The effort, like scientific endeavors, is to establish truth. Once enough evidence is presented which disproves an old theory, then a new hypothesis is developed, challenged and refined. Our old concepts of history, archeology and geology must become more flexible so that we can truly understand the history of man. And with this improved information, we should be able to make better judgments as to how to operate in the future. ❖

Ronald P. Anjard is an internationally recognized authority on philosophical and technological subjects. This article was originally published in the Fall 1977 issue of The American Mercury, *then owned by TBR publisher, Willis A. Carto.*

This photo of a Mandan Indian tribal gathering was taken in 1970. By 1971, there were no more full-blooded Mandans left upon whom genetic testing could be conducted. When the first modern European explorers of the upper American Midwest came across the Mandans, they were struck by the European features of many tribal members.

THE ENIGMATIC ORIGINS OF THE MANDAN INDIANS

BY JOHN TIFFANY

Scholars have been debating for a generation the mysterious origins of the Mandan Indians, a group of Amerinds that lived in the north-central region of the United States. Many of the members of the Mandan tribe had blue eyes, light hair, and spoke a language that strongly resembled Old Welsh, though classified in the Siouan family.

Around the time of the death of Owain Gwynedd (A.D. 1169), the great prince of Wales, fierce rivalry among the sons of his several wives broke out, as they fought for supremacy over north Wales. One of the younger sons, however, Madoc the Bold, is said to have decided to leave his homeland and to sail away in search of the legendary fountain of youth.

From a small harbor at the mouth of the River Ganol on the north coast of Wales, Prince Madoc and his men put out to sea, sailing into the sunset.

After many days Madoc returned to Wales, spinning yarns of deep and dangerous waters where ships became entangled in a garden of yellow seaweed, of huge fish that got away, and of a

This portrait of a Mandan woman, Me-Nwek-E-Sunk-To-Ka, by George Cat-lin, shows the affinities of this North American tribe with the people of Europe. Shown at right is the framework of a Mandan coracle or "koorig," as it was called in their language. The Welsh word for coracle is "corwg," pronounced "corrug."

strange but fruitful country where the native people had red skins and black hair.

Then the prince and his brother Rhiryd, lord of Clochran, collected together such men and women as desired to try a new life, and they set sail from the Island of Lundy in 10 small ships to establish a Welsh colony in an unknown land.

Nothing more was seen or heard in Wales of Madoc and his ships. Columbus rediscovered America 300 years later. The Spanish reported with surprise that some of the natives were already worshipping the Christian cross.

Later explorers discovered an unusual tribe of Indians living on the banks of the Missouri. Their skin was fair, and their hair

"Bull-boats," made by stretching buffalo hides over frames of light wood, are clearly seen in the foreground of this sketch of a 19th-century Mandan village on the Missouri River in North Dakota. These boats are very similar to the "currachs" of the Irish or the coracles of the Welsh people. Interestingly, many early European travelers claimed that Indians they ran into spoke a form of Welsh. Did the Indians get both their language and their nautical technology from ancient Kelts who came to America before Columbus?

was blond, red or brown.

These Indians called themselves Mandans. They peppered their language with Welsh words and fished from boats made like the coracles of Wales. They told how their tribe had once dwelt at the mouth of three rivers on the Gulf of Mexico, from where they had made a long trek north to the Knife River on the Upper Missouri.

The Welsh Indians lived in settlements built on rocky outcrops that resembled the so-called "hill forts" of Britain. Their lodges looked like beehives and were made of timber, plastered thickly with earth. These huts were grouped into large villages defended by palisades, ramparts and ditches, and each village was surrounded by regular patterns of fields growing crops.

They treasured most highly the possession of blue glass beads—the kind of beads used in trade by seamen from the Island of Lundy.

Every Mandan village harbored a "holy canoe" made out of red cedar, around which rituals and ceremonial dances were performed. This shrine was dedicated to the "Lone White Man," who had brought the Mandans in his big canoe from across the great water.

Some Mandan women, especially, possessed almost Nordic features—characteristics clearly shown in frontier pictorial historian George Catlin's portraits of Sha-Ko-Ka ("Mint") and Me-Nwek-E-Sunk-To-Ka (shown on page 134). Apart from their Indian clothing, these women might have been mistaken for Europeans. Catlin described Mandan women as having "a mildness and sweetness of expression, and excessive modesty of demeanor," rendering them "exceedingly pleasing and beautiful." He found Mandans in general to be "a very interesting and pleasing people in their personal appearance and manners, differing in many respects, both in looks and customs, from all the other tribes I have seen."   ❖

ANCIENT CHINESE & JAPANESE GOT TO AMERICA, TOO?

Did cultured Asiatics arrive in the Americas before Columbus? Illustration 1: A round-bellied, almond-eyed Mexican terra-cotta figure (1400-1150 B.C.) that could pass for a modern-day sumo wrestler. 2: An Incan ruler appears in state with two symbols of Andean power— the litter and the parasol. In Asia too, these privileges were granted only to the elite. 3: A Moche ceramic vessel. Depicted is a fisherman retrieving a fish from a restrained bird. Japanese fishermen have been known to use cormorants in this way for centuries. 4: A bearded, Chinese-looking basalt figure carved by the Olmecs of Central America and known as "the wrestler," surely hints at a real-life model.

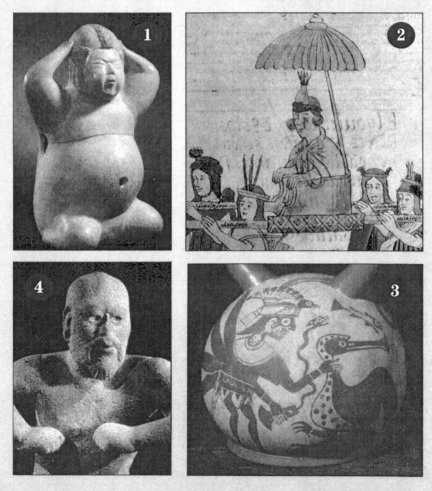

Above, an artist's conception of an encounter between Vikings and Skrael-ings. Vikings did much of their exploring and trading in knarrs, deeper drafted merchant vessels that could hold more cargo than the classic low-draft Viking longboat. The depiction of the two men with winged helmets (one helmet has fallen off) is probably inaccurate. Scholars almost unanimously agree that Vikings wore neither wings nor horns on their helmets although one horned helmet was found in a Viking grave. Such helmets were probably used only during ceremonial occasions.

Researcher Robert Ellis Cahill identifies this item as a Viking axe head found in Nova Scotia. Another, very much like, it was found in Plymouth, Massachusetts.

THORFINN KARLSEFNI'S VOYAGE TO NORTH AMERICA

TRANSLATED FROM *THE SAGA OF ERIK THE RED*

Although the legendary sagas of the Norsemen are rife with exaggeration and folklore, they are still looked upon by many scholars as first-hand accounts of the voyages of the Vikings. Many of the descriptions of the flora and fauna they saw and the geographical details have led researchers to conclude that much of the sagas is an accurate description of voyages to the New World. Here, part of *The Saga of Erik the Red* is reproduced so that you can hear from the ancient people themselves about their experiences in the New World, probably Newfoundland.

There was a man named Thorfinn Karlsefni, the son of Thord Horsehead, who lived in north Iceland, at the place now called Reynines in Skagafjord. Karlsefni was a man of good family and good means. His mother was named Thorunn. He went on trading voyages and was a merchant of good repute.

(Karlsefni, actually a nickname, means "makings of a man," which he had aplenty.)

One summer Karlsefni made his ship ready for a voyage to

Greenland. Snorri Thorbrandsson of Alftafjord was to accompany him, and they took a party of 40 men with them.

A man named Bjarni Grimolfsson, from Breidafjord, and another named Thorhall Gamlason, from the East Fjords, made their ship ready the same summer as Karlsefni and were also heading for Greenland. There were 40 men on their ship. The two ships set sail once they had made ready.

There is no mention of how long they were at sea. But it is said that both these ships sailed into Eriksfjord that autumn.

Erik [the Red] rode to the ships, along with other Greenlanders, and busy trading commenced. The skippers of the vessels invited Erik to take his pick of their wares, and Erik repaid them in Brattahlid, Erik's estate in the "Eastern Settlement." This the merchants accepted and went home with him. Their goods were later transported to Brattahlid, where there was no lack of good and ample outbuildings to store them in. The merchants were highly pleased with their winter stay with Erik.

After Yule Karlsefni approached Erik to ask for Gudrid's hand, as it seemed to him that she was under Erik's protection, and both an attractive and knowledgeable woman. Erik answered that he would support his suit, and that she was a fine match "and it's likely that her fate will turn out as prophesied" [that she would marry an Icelander and that they would have a long life together with many descendants.—Ed]. The subject was broached with Gudrid and she allowed herself to be guided by Erik's advice. No more needs to be said on that point, except the match was agreed and the celebrations extended to include the wedding, which took place.

That winter there was much merrymaking and feasting in Brattahlid; many board games were played, there was storytelling and plenty of other entertainment to brighten the life of the household.

There were great discussions that winter in Brattahlid of Snorri and Karlsefni setting sail for Vinland. In the end Snorri and

Karlsefni made their vessel ready, intending to sail in search of Vinland that summer. Bjarni and Thorhall decided to accompany them on the voyage, taking their own ship and their own companions who had sailed with them on the voyage out.

A man named Thorvard was married to Freydis, who was an illegitimate daughter of Erik the Red. He went with them, along with Thorvald, Erik's son, and Thorhall, who was called "the Huntsman." For years he had accompanied Erik on hunting trips in the summers, and was entrusted with many tasks. Thorhall was a large man, dark and coarse-featured; he was getting on in years and difficult to handle. He was a silent man, who was not generally given to conversation, devious and yet insulting in his speech, and who usually did his best to make trouble. He had paid scant heed to the Christian faith since it had come to Greenland. Thorhall was not popular with most people, but he had long been in Erik's confidence. He was among those on the ship with Thorvald and Thorvard, as he had a wide knowledge of the uninhabited regions. They had the ship which Thorbjorn had brought to Greenland and set sail with Karlsefni and his group. Most of the men aboard were from Greenland. The crews of the three ships made 140 men.

They sailed along the coast to the Western Settlement, then to Bear Island and from there with a northly wind. After two days at sea they sighted land and rowed over in boats to explore it. There they found many flat slabs of stone, so large that two men could lie foot-to-foot across them. There were many foxes there. They gave the land the name Helluland [Stone-slab land].

After that they sailed with a northerly wind for two days, and again sighted land, with large forests and many animals. An island lay to the southeast, off the coast, where they discovered a bear, and they called it Bjarney [Bear Island], and the forested land itself Markland.

After another two days passed they again sighted land and approached the shore where a peninsula jutted out. They sailed upwind along the coast, keeping the land on the starboard. The country was wild with a long shoreline and sand flats. They rowed ashore in boats and, discovering the keel of a ship there, named this point Kjalarnes [Keel Point]. They also gave the beaches the name Furdustrandir [Wonder Beaches] for their surprising length. After this the coastline was indented with numerous inlets, which they skirted in their ships.

When Leif had served King Olaf Tryggvason and was told by him to convert Greenland to Christianity, the king had given him two Scots, a man named Haki and a woman called Hekja. The king told him to call upon them whenever he needed someone with speed, as they were fleeter of foot than any deer. Leif and Erik had sent them to accompany Karlsefni.

After sailing the length of the Furdustrandir, they put the two Scots ashore and told them to run southward to explore the country and return before three day's time had elapsed. They were dressed in a garment known as a *kjafal*, which had a hood at the top but no arms, and was open at the sides and fastened between the legs with a button and loop; they wore nothing else. The ships cast anchor and lay to during this time.

After three days had passed the two returned to the shore, one of them with grapes in hand and the other with self-sown wheat. Karlsefni said that they had found good land. After taking them on board once more, they sailed onward, until they reached a fjord cutting into the coast. They steered the ships into the fjord with an island near its mouth, where there were strong currents, and called the island Straumsey [Stream Island]. There were so many birds there that they could hardly walk without stepping on eggs. They sailed up a small river, which they called Straumsfjord, unloaded the cargo from the ships and began settling in.

They had brought all sorts of livestock with them and explored the land and its resources. There were mountains there, and a pleasant landscape. They paid little attention to things other than exploring the land. The grass there grew tall.

They spent the winter there, and it was a harsh winter, for which they had made little preparation, and they grew short of food and caught nothing when hunting and fishing. They went out to the island, expecting to find some prey to hunt or food on the beaches. They found little food, but their livestock improved there.

After this they entreated God to send them something to eat, but the response was not as quick incoming as their need was urgent. Thorhall disappeared, and men went to look for him. They searched for three days, and on the fourth Karlsefni and Bjarni found him at the edge of a cliff. He was staring skywards, with his mouth, nostrils and eyes wide open, scratching and pinching himself and mumbling something.

They asked what he was doing there, and he replied that it made no difference. He said they need not look so surprised and said for most of his life he had got along without their advice. They told him to come back with them, and he did so.

Shortly afterward they found a beached whale and flocked to the site to carve it up, although they failed to recognize what type it was. Karlsefni had a wide knowledge of whales, but even he did not recognize it. The cooks boiled the meat, and they ate it, but it made everyone ill.

Thorhall then came up and spoke: "Didn't Old Redbeard prove to be more help than your Christ? This was my payment for the poem I composed about Thor, my guardian, who's seldom disappointed me."

Once they heard this no one wanted to eat the whale meat, they cast it off a cliff and threw themselves on God's mercy. The weather improved so they could go fishing, and from then on they had supplies.

In the spring they moved further into Straumsfjord and lived on the produce of both shores of the fjord, hunting game inland, gathering eggs on the island and fishing at sea.

They then began to discuss and plan the continuation of their journey. Thorhall wanted to head north, past Furdustrandir and around Kjalarnes, to seek Vinland. Karlsefni wished to sail south along the east shore, feeling the land would be more substantial the farther south it was, and he felt it was advisable to explore both.

Thorhall then made his ship ready close to the island, with no more than nine men to accompany him. The rest of their company went with Karlsefni.

After that they set out, and Karlsefni followed them.

They then separated and Thorhall and his crew sailed north past Furdustrandir and Kjalarnes, and from there attempted to sail to the west of it. But they ran into storms and were driven ashore in Ireland, where they were beaten and enslaved. There Thorhall died.

Karlsefni headed south around the coast, with Snorri and Bjarni and the rest of their company. They sailed a long time, until they came to a river, which flowed into a lake and from there into the sea. There were wide sandbars beyond the mouth of the river, and they could only sail into the river at high tide. Karlsefni and his company sailed into the lagoon and called the land Hop [Tidal Pool]. There they found fields of self-sown wheat in the low-lying areas and vines growing in the hills. Every stream was teeming with fish. They dug trenches along the high-water mark, and when the tide ebbed there were halibut[1] in them. There were a great number of deer of all kinds in the forest.

They stayed there for a forenight, enjoying themselves and finding nothing unusual. They had taken their livestock with them.

Early one morning they noticed nine hide-covered boats, and

the people in them waved wooden poles that made a swishing sound as they turned them around sunwise.

Karlsefni spoke: "What can this mean?"

Snorri replied: "It may be a sign of peace; we should take a white shield and lift it up in return."

This they did, and the others then rowed toward them and were astonished at the sight of them as they landed on the shore. They were short in height with threatening features and tangled hair on their heads. Their eyes were large and their cheeks broad. They stayed there awhile, marvelling, then rowed away again to the south around the point.

The group had built their booths up above the lake, with some of the huts farther inland, and others close to the shore.

They remained there that winter. There was no snow at all, and the livestock could fend for themselves out of doors.

One morning, as spring advanced, they noticed a large number of hide-covered boats rowing up from the south around the point. There were so many of them that it looked as if bits of coal had been tossed over the water, and there was a pole waving from each boat. They signalled with their shields and began trading with the visitors, who mostly wished to trade for red cloth. They also wanted to purchase swords and spears, but Karlsefni and Snorri forbade this. They traded dark pelts for the cloth, and for each pelt they took cloth a hand in length, which they bound about their heads.

This went on for some time, until there was little cloth left. They then cut the cloth into smaller pieces, each no wider than a finger's width, but the natives gave just as much for it or more.

At this point a bull, owned by Karlsefni and his companions, ran out of the forest and bellowed loudly. The natives took fright at this, ran to their boats and rowed off to the south. Three weeks passed and there was no sign of them.

After that they saw a large group of native boats approaching from the south, as thick as a steady stream. They were waving poles counter-sunwise now and all of them were shrieking loudly. The men took up their red shields and went toward them. They met and began fighting. A hard barrage rained down, and the natives also had catapults. [Possibly slingshots—Ed.] Karlsefni and Snorri then saw the natives lift up on poles a large round object, about the size of a sheep's gut and black in color, which came flying up on the land and made a threatening noise when it landed. It struck great fear into Karlsefni and his men, who decided their best course was to flee upriver, since the native party seemed to be attacking from all sides, until they reached a cliff wall where they could put up a good fight.

Fredyis came out of the camp as they were fleeing. She called, "Why do you flee such miserable opponents, men like you who look to me to be capable of killing them off like sheep? Had I a weapon I'm sure I would fight better than any of you." They paid no attention to what she said. Fredyis wanted to go with them, but moved somewhat slowly, as she was with child. She followed them into the forest, but the natives reached her. She came across a slain man, Thorbrand Snorrason, who had been struck in the head by a slab of stone. His sword lay beside him, and this she snatched up and prepared to defend herself with it as the natives approached her. Freeing one of her breasts from her shift, she smacked the sword with it. This frightened the natives, who turned and ran back to their boats and rowed away.

Karlsefni and his men came back to her and praised her luck.

Two of Karlsefni's men were killed, and many of the natives were slain, yet Karlsefni and his men were outnumbered. They returned to the booths wondering who these numerous people were who attacked them on land. But it now looked to them as if the company in the booths had been the sole attackers, and any other attackers had only been an illusion.

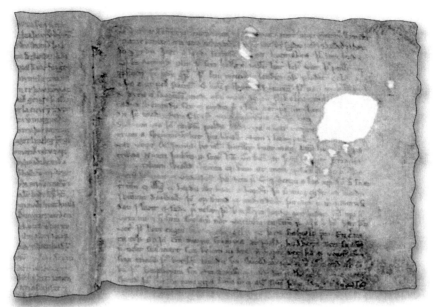

This portion of a page from Erik the Red's Saga *describes an encounter between Vikings and "Skraelings," as the Vikings called the Amerinds and Eskimos. Although winners in this encounter, the Norse decided it was wise to return home.*

The natives also found one of the dead men, whose axe lay beside him. One of them picked up the axe and chopped at a tree, and then each took his turn at it. They thought this thing which cut so well a real treasure. One of them struck a stone and the axe broke. He thought a thing which could not withstand stone to be of little worth, and tossed it away. [Metal Viking axe heads have been found as far south as Massachusetts—Ed.]

The party then realized that, despite everything the land had to offer there, they would be under constant threat of attack from its prior inhabitants. They made ready to depart for their own country. Sailing north along the shore, they discovered five natives sleeping in skin sacks near the shore. Beside them they had vessels filled with deer marrow blended with blood. They assumed these men to be outlaws and killed them.

They then came to a headland thick with deer. The point looked like a huge dunghill, as the deer gathered there at night to sleep. They then entered Straumsfjord, where they found food in plenty. Some people say that Bjarni and Gudrid had remained behind there with a hundred others and gone no farther, and that it was Karlsefni and Snorri who went farther south with some 40 men, stayed no more than two months at Hop and returned the same summer.

The group stayed there while Karlsefni went on one ship to look for Thorhall. They sailed north around Kjalarnes Point and then westward of it, keeping the land on their port side. They saw nothing but wild forest. When they had sailed for a long time they reached a river flowing from east to west. They sailed into the mouth of the river and lay to near the south bank.

One morning Karlsefni's men saw something shiny above the clearing in the trees, and they called out. It moved and proved to be a one-legged creature which darted down to where the ship lay tied. Thorvald, Erik the Red's son, was at the helm, and the one-legged man shot an arrow into his intestine. Thorvald drew the arrow out and spoke: "Fat paunch that was. We've found a land of fine resources, though we've hardly enjoyed much of them." Thorvald died from the wound shortly after. The one-legged man then ran off back north. [Was this a native in an animal-hide skirt? One-legged men can't run very well.—Ed.] They pursued him and caught glimpses of him now and again. He then fled into a cove, and they turned back.

They soon left to head northward where they thought they sighted the Land of the One-Legged, but did not want to put their lives in further danger. They saw mountains which they felt to be the same as those near Hop, and both these places seemed to be equally far away from Straumsfjord.

They returned to spend their third winter in Straumsfjord.

Many quarrels arose, as the men who had no wives sought to take those of the married men. Karlsefni's son Snorri was born there the first autumn and was three years old when they left.

They had southerly winds and reached Markland, where they met five natives. One was bearded, two were women and two of them children. [Possibly a group from a Christian Keltic settlement. There is much evidence of an ancient Keltic presence in the Northeast.—Ed.] Karlsefni and his men caught the boys but the others escaped and disappeared into the earth. They took the boys with them and taught them their language and had them baptized. They called their mother Vethild and their father Ovaegi. They said that kings ruled the land of the natives; one of them was called Avaldamon and the other Valdidida. No houses were there, they said, but people slept in caves or holes. [Possibly the characteristic underground chambers and dwellings that ancient people from the British Isles were well known for building and which abound in New England.—Ed.] They spoke of another land, across the water from their own. There people dressed in white clothing, shouted loudly and bore poles and waved banners. This, people assumed, was the land of the white men.[2] [Possibly a Christian Keltic processional. Christian Keltic rock carvings and shrines have been found by researchers in significant numbers in the Northeast. [One such site is Gungywamp, Connecticut, although there are more—Ed.]

They then came to Greenland and spent the winter with Erik the Red.

Bjarni Grimolfsson and his group were born into the Greenland Straits and entered Madkasjo [Sea of Worms], although they failed to realize it until the ship under them had become infested with shipworms. They then discussed what to do. They had a ship's boat in tow, which had been smeared with tar made of seal blubber. It is said that shell maggots cannot infest wood smeared with such tar. The majority proposed to set as many men into the boat as it could carry. When this was tried, it turned out to have room for no more than half of them.

Bjarni then said they should decide by lot who should go in the boat, and not decide by status. Although all of the people there wanted to go into the boat, it couldn't take them all. The outcome was that it fell to Bjarni and almost half of those on board to go in the boat. Those who had been selected left the ship and boarded the boat.

Once they were aboard the boat one young Icelander, who had sailed with Bjarni, called out to him, "Are you going to desert me now, Bjarni?"

"So it must be," Bjarni answered.

He said, "That's not what you promised me when I left my father's house in Iceland to follow you."

Bjarni answered, "I don't see we've much other choice now. What would you advise?"

He said, "I see the solution—that we change places, you come up here and I'll take your place there."

"So be it," Bjarni answered, "as I see you put a high price on life and are very upset about dying."

They then changed places. The man climbed into the boat and Bjarni aboard the ship. People say Bjarni died there in the Sea of Worms, along with the others on board his ship. The ship's boat and those on it went on their way and made land, after which they told this tale. And here ends this saga.   ❖

ENDNOTES:

1 Although the Icelandic term *helgir fiskar* (literally "holy fishes") means "halibut" in English, these could be any type of flatfish.

2 Some scholars have suggested this refers to American Indians, others to a Christian ceremony, as the term "white men" was used for Christians. One manuscript supplies the explanation that it refers to "Ireland the Great."

PHOENICIANS HERE TOO?

ABOVE, THIS PIECE OF ENGRAVED ROCK is known as the Bourne Stone, found in Massachusetts. Diffusionist and world-renowned epigrapher Barry Fell interpreted the writing on the stone to be an annexation of the region for Carthage (a major Phoenician city-state in north Africa) by a Phoenician named Hanno, who may have been the same Carthaginian suffete of the same name and approximate period.

THIS PRE-COLUMBIAN INCENSE BURNER portrays a bearded face with Semitic features. It was found in Guatemala in the last century. Some scholars speculate that the Mesoamerican artist must have actually encountered this Middle Eastern-looking individual.

THIS ENGRAVED TABLET, above, inscribed in Iberian script and employing the Punic language, shares some of its vocabulary and all its basic styles and characters with the historic tablet of Tasach, excavated in 1838 from the foot of the Mammoth Mound at Moundsville. It was found in a stream bed in central West Virginia, and was first thought to be of Viking origin. This stone has been interpreted to read as follows: "The memorial of Teth, this tile his brother caused to be made."

RIGHT, THIS STONE IS KNOWN AS THE PONTOTOC STELE. It was found by amateur archeologist Gloria Farley in Oklahoma and is apparently the work of an early Iberian Punic colonist in America. The script is that known otherwise only from the Cachao-da-Rapa region in northern Portugal. The stone depicts the life-giving rays of the sun descending upon the earth beneath. To the left, the Iberian Punic letters spell "Start of Dawn," to the right "Dusk," with the crescent-ship of the Moon.

ABOVE, THIS STONE was found by prominent diffusionist James Whittall of the Early Sites Research Foundation, who has collected and deciphered such objects for decades in New England. It was found in a small rectangular stone chamber at the Mystery Hill, New Hampshire megalithic site. The chamber has since been identified as a winter solstice observatory, although the establishment still insists the rambling stone complex at Mystery Hill is nothing more than a collection of colonial root cellars. The markings of the stone have been interpreted by epigraphers as Iberian Punic and read: "To Baal of the Canaanites (Phoenicians), this in dedication." Other establishmentarians still insist the markings are merely scrapes left behind by plows or the action of roots. (Note: Markings have been accentuated with white pigment.)

According to APS—Scott Wolter's American Petrographic Services—(a company that specializes in "material forensics"), the controversial Kensington Rune Stone was obviously prepared for the inscription by first splitting the stone along natural fault lines. The glacial sides of the stone (characterized by scratches caused by the ice sheet), which were not split by human effort, exhibit only slightly more weathering than the two inscribed sides, according to APS. Shown above is the "face side" of the stone, one of the glaciated surfaces. Shown below is one of the more narrow "split sides," where it was broken off by humans from the mother slab of rock. Runic inscriptions are clearly seen on both of these surfaces. The inscription starts on the front, and continues on the split side. According to APS, these two surfaces are the only non-glaciated sides of the stone. The top, bottom, back and one of the two narrower sides are all glaciated.

THE KENSINGTON RUNE STONE: A MINNESOTA MYSTERY SOLVED

By Stephen J. Martin

Even the establishment now admits that Leif Eriksson and other Vikings reached at least as far as what is now Canada and made settlements there. But controversy continues to surround claims that the Vikings penetrated to Minnesota, perhaps by way of Hudson Bay. The main evidence that they may have done so is the Kensington Rune Stone (KRS). But the stone has been widely pooh-poohed. Is it real, or is it a fake? Is the famous and oft-debated artifact a legitimate historical record of the travels of Scandinavian adventurers into the heartland of America in the mid-14th century? Some new developments have proved conclusively to all but the most stodgy establishmentarian academics the absolute legitimacy of the KRS.

Recent advances in the understanding of the Kensington Rune Stone consist of a conclusive paper on the linguistic aspects of the runes and the words used by the carver and an equally irrefutable study of the geological aspects of the stone itself. Less has occurred recently within the third milieu, that of historical documentation from elsewhere—yet, nothing has been found to challenge the spectacular advances within the past few months in the century-old effort to exonerate the KRS from the hasty and ill-informed initial opinions of skeptics. Perhaps the most impressive indicator of the importance of recent advances has been the almost total silence from the KRS's nay-sayers. In the past, claims by proponents of the stone's legitimacy were almost always countered, often very quickly, by an army of court historians desperate to prop up their ill-conceived and erroneous notions of the progression of New World exploration and settlement by Europeans.

The linguistic advances have come in the form of an exhaustive 74-page article by Dr. Richard Neilsen in the journal *Scandinavian Studies* (spring 2001). This paper annihilates all of the linguistic objections made against the KRS on the basis of supposedly modern grammar and word forms found within the inscription. It also answers all of the previous complaints directed toward some of the rune forms utilized throughout the 74-word message as being unavailable in the 14th century. Dr. Neilsen has a broad résumé of both academic achievement and life experience (as opposed to purely academic insularity and narrow-mindedness), which establishes his ability to speak authoritatively on the linguistic aspects of the stone. He began his career after graduation from the Coast Guard Academy as a member of a 1957 circumnavigation of the Arctic Ocean in search of a deep water channel. He earned an M.S.E. in ship design from the University of Michigan in 1961, and an M.S. in mathematics from that same institution in 1964. He earned a doctorate of technology from the University of Denmark in Copenhagen in 1965.

He became fluent in Danish and began a nearly 40-year infatuation with Scandinavian cultures and languages. He then went into the oil exploration business, which took him to 150 countries, where he became conversant in many languages. Returning to Scandinavia for various stints (Oslo in 1978, Denmark in 1979-82 and again in 1983-85), he continued his study of Scandinavian languages and became fluent in Norwegian, Swedish, Finnish and Icelandic. As an employee of the Bechtel Corporation back in the States (1985-87), he continued to be sent back to the region three times per year and kept his languages fresh by examining and studying various Scandinavian artifacts and ancient writings in his spare time.

Early in his examination of the KRS, Dr. Neilsen was able to eliminate the old objection to the KRS pertaining to the appearance of an Arabic "10" in the inscription. This was just one of many usages that scholars (beginning with Prof. O.J. Breda at the University of Minnesota in 1899[1]) with their limited knowledge of forms available to 14th century Scandinavian scholars and clerics had used to bolster their contention that the inscription was a modern forgery. Dr. Neilsen pointed out many years ago (and within two weeks of his first examination of the KRS) that the medieval Scandinavians had translated a huge Arabic text on mathematics by the 14th century,[2] a fact then unknown to detractors. This piqued Neilsen's interest in the KRS controversy and initiated a decade-long study of the stone and its fascinating message.

In his previously mentioned paper, Neilsen takes all of the other criticisms and devastates them by showing in detail how each of the supposedly modern forms appears in ancient writings that predate the KRS elsewhere across Scandinavia. Many of these sources were also apparently unknown to, or at least never utilized by, the critics. While a complete summary of his masterful silencing of the critics is beyond the scope of this paper, a couple of examples will suffice.

One of the major criticisms of the KRS inscription prior to the Neilsen article had been the supposed appearance of the word "*opdagelse*" (a word meaning "discovery") that critics have always said did not appear in the Scandinavian lexicons until many decades after the 1362 date in the KRS inscription. Neilsen points out in his paper that the correct translation ought to have been "*opthagelse*," meaning "acquisition." The problem lay once again with early 20th-century limitations in the understanding of medieval rune forms. The rune for "th" had been incorrectly transliterated "d" for decades. Neilsen's most up-to-date translation, as provided by the curator of the Rune Stone Museum in Alexandria, Minnesota,[3] now reads:

Eight Goths and 202 Northmen are on acquisition business from Vinland far to the west. We had encampment by two shelters one day's time north from this stone we were fishing one day. After we came home I found 10 men red from blood and dead (death). Hail Mary deliver from evil. I have 10 men by the sea to attend to our ship 14 days' journey from this wealth. Year of Christ 1362.

The next example consists of the strenuous objections regarding the appearance of double dots throughout the text of the inscription. Critics smugly pointed out that the Germanic umlaut did not come into usage until well after 1362. Dr. Neilsen shows[1] that these are properly understood as word-break markers, used to signify where one word ends and another begins. The article contains many startling and exciting discoveries of this type. In short, Neilsen's work eliminates any objection from a linguistic perspective to the inscription being precisely what it purports to be—a frantic record of a besieged party of Scandinavians in the center of the North American continent 130 years before Columbus.

Other developments within the field of geology—when combined with Dr. Neilsen's thus far unchallenged linguistic work—serve as the second of back-to-back homers in the bottom of the ninth (after being down one) for supporters of the KRS's legitimacy. Scott Wolter of American Petrographic Services got his degree in geology from the University of Minnesota-Duluth in 1982. In 1990, he founded a company that specializes in material forensics. Engineers, architects and municipalities are the chief customers of the firm, which has done extensive microscopic examination of the stone and begun the process of chemical analysis, which should have been started decades ago. The majority of geologists who have examined the KRS over the years have either gone on record in favor of its authenticity or adopted a wait-and-see attitude. This is in stark contrast to the linguistic academicians, who have merely echoed, for the most part, the initial errant conclusions of their forebears up to the present.

Twelve years after Olof Ohman found the stone entangled beneath the tree roots of a 40- to 70-year-old poplar at his farm in Kensington, Minnesota, the Midwest's most prominent geologist, Prof. N.H. Winchell, put his signature to a document of a committee put together by the Minnesota Historical Society for the purpose of examining the stone. The report, dated April 21, 1910, reads:

> **Resolved, that this committee renders a favorable opinion of the authenticity of the Kensington Rune Stone, provided that the references to Scandinavian literature given in this committee's report and accompanying papers be verified by a competent specialist in the Scandinavian languages. . . .**[5]

Given that Dr. Neilsen has, 91 years later, finally provided the answer to the committee's caveat, it remains only to echo and expand earlier geological opinions with state-of-the-art examination techniques. Before doing so, two more quotes from the same era as Winchell's committee serve to set the tone for understanding the geologic community's response to the KRS to date. Prof. W.O. Hotchkiss, then state geologist of Wisconsin, wrote (also in 1910) the following:

> **I have carefully examined the various phases of weathering on the Kensington Stone, and with all respect for the opinions of philologists, I am persuaded that the inscription could not have been made in recent years. It must have been made at least 50 to 100 years ago and perhaps earlier.**[6]

This statement is extremely important in light of the fact that the first white settlers from Scandinavia (the most frequent targets of the forgery theorists) did not settle in that part of Minnesota until much after 50 years prior to the stone's discovery in the fall of 1898.

The geologists' qualification of their statements is understandable in light of the well-written (though now thoroughly moot) objections of skeptics. It took just as much courage to overrule the considered opinions of a phalanx of linguistic Ph.D.s in 1910 as it does for heroes like Neilsen and Wolter to do so today. After all, reputations built over many years are not easily gambled in the court of established academic opinion, given the well-known resistance to new discoveries that may challenge outdated notions.

Another early examination of the stone was undertaken by Dr. Warren Upham, an eminent glacial geologist. In 1910 he wrote:

When we compare the excellent preservation of the glacial scratches, shown on the back of the stone, which were made several thousand years ago, with the mellow, time-worn appearance of the face of the inscription, the conclusion is inevitable that this inscription must have been carved hundreds of years ago.[7]

Such is the tenor of the opinions of the early 20th-century geologists who examined the KRS.

This author knows of no eminent geologist who has published any documentation of a viewpoint critical of Winchell, Hotchkiss and Upham within the last 100+ years. Most geologists have simply refused to study the KRS as a result of the widely held and widely publicized negative opinions of the philologists. Enter Scott Wolter and American Petrographics. The results of geological analysis of the stone ought to be given far more weight in the discussion than any of the linguistic arguments, either pro or con. If the inscription can be proved to have been written prior to the 1830s—when the first white explorers of the modern era began to traverse central Minnesota on their way to points farther west—it makes no difference whether Olof Ohman had a book with some runes in it inside his farmhouse, or that papers about Scandinavian explorations to America predating Columbus may have been available to the Scandinavian settlers of Douglas County, Minnesota. It also matters not how numerous and well devised the arguments in favor of a possible forger put forth by detractors such as Erik Wahlgren in his *The Kensington Stone: A Mystery Solved* (University of Wisconsin Press, 1958) might be. Unless Wahlgren, and others. would argue that the American Indians had obtained an in-depth knowledge of medieval Norse by some divine revelation, the KRS could only have been made by just the type of people mentioned in the translation of the inscription.

Scott Wolter was asked by Luann Patten of the Rune Stone Museum in July of 2000 to conduct forensic analysis of the KRS in keeping with standard scientific procedure. Wolter told this writer in an interview by telephone that he had never heard of the KRS prior to this request, and entered the project with no preconceptions either for or against its authenticity.

The 30-page APS report concludes with these words:

It is clear that the manmade surface types on the KRS exhibit weathering (primarily mica degradation) consistent with being buried in the ground for at least decades and probably centuries. This being the case, the logical conclusion is that the KRS is an authentic artifact, presumably made at the time it is dated.

Wolter says that his observations are conclusive, with regard to the above statements. However, he makes some suggestions for further study that might be helpful in pinpointing the age of the inscriptions with more accuracy. These suggestions include:

1) Tombstone studies to quantify the rate of mica decomposition: Gravestones of incremental known ages (5, 10, 25, 50, 100, 200 years) should be sampled for analysis using scanning electron microscope (SEM) in order to generate a timeline for mica degradation that could be used for dating the

Kensington Rune Stone inscriptions.

2) Location studies with the goal of identifying the bedrock source of the KRS graywacke: Samples taken from the bedrock source would then be used in accelerated weather testing (to include an autoclave and a freeze-thaw chamber). Chips should then be subjected to reflected light microscopy and SEM.

3) The data achieved above (#2) should then be analyzed with the intent of projecting a mica-degradation timeline and a weathering time line to be compared with the results from suggestion #1.

4) A thorough microscopic digital photo library of the entire inscription should be produced under various magnifications.

5) A qualified plant specialist should be consulted to examine the chemical processes and timing involved to develop the root bleaching observed on the back side of the KRS.

It appears that Olof Ohman, his descendants and the early defenders of the stone—such as Hjalmar Holand (who purchased the stone from Ohman and wrote several books on the subject) and Prof. Robert Hall, whose classic work *The Kensington Rune Stone Is Genuine* (Columbia: Hornbeam Press, 1982) anticipated Neilsen—have finally been fully vindicated. The Ohman family, to the fourth generation, still bears the onus of rebuke from dozens of neighbors and academic skeptics who now owe them a full apology for their crass and insensitive insinuations. Cognizant Americans should now put the Kensington Rune Stone in the place it deserves in our nation's history. The little museum in Alexandria, Minn. now deserves to be on everyone's travel itinerary as much as does Plymouth Rock.

For those interested in further reading on this topic, Holand's most interesting book (*Westward from Vinland*, New York: Duell, Sloan & Pearce, 1940), on a possible historical explanation for why the Kensington Rune Stone carvers may have been in the American heartland in 1362, is a must. Interested individuals should also visit the websites of current researchers such as the Massey twins (Keith and Kevin), Michael Zalar and Yuri Kuchinsky. ❖

FOOTNOTES:
1 Wahlgren, 17.
2 Neilsen, interviewed by telephone, September 5, 2001.
3 Brochure from Rune Stone Museum, Alexandria, Minn.
4 Neilsen, 6.
5 Holand, 105.
6 In *ibid.*, 130.
7 *Ibid.*

BIBLIOGRAPHY:
Holand, Hjalmar, *Westward from Vinland: An Account of Norse Discoveries and Explorations in America, 982-1362*, New York: Duell, Sloan & Pearce, 1940.
Neilsen, Dr. Richard, "A Response to Dr. James Knirk's Essay on the Kensington Rune Stone," in the spring 2001 edition of *Scandinavian Studies*, Vol. 72, No. 1.
Wahlgren, Erik, *The Kensington Stone: A Mystery Solved*, Madison, Wis.: University of Wisconsin Press, 1958.

Stephen J. Martin is a political activist and pianist and is a native of Pennsylvania who resides in Maine. Steve, a former teacher with a deep interest in politics, ran for state representative for Maine's 141st district, but narrowly lost.

In 1898, Swedish immigrant farmer Olof Ohman discovered a 202-lb. tablet engraved with runes while working the fields on his Douglas County, Minnesota, property. Ohman believed the stone was proof that Vikings were in America before Christopher Columbus, but was quickly ruled to be a fraudster. He suffered greatly from the smears but now has been vindicated posthumously.

RUNE STONE DECODED: VIKINGS, TEMPLARS & GOTHS IN AMERICA IN 1362

BY FRANK JOSEPH

When a simple immigrant farmer discovered what seemed to be an ancient stone with "Viking-style" runes inscribed on it in Minnesota, people said he was crazy or lying. But more than 100 years later, additional discoveries have proved the stele was indeed the real McCoy, although left there by Knights Templar of the Middle Ages rather than Thor-worshipping Norsemen.

Very few books are truly capable of rewriting history, but *The Hooked X: Key to the Secret History of North America*, by Scott F. Wolter, is certainly one of them. Although the author of this Revisionist book, who is well known to longtime readers of TBR, is a professional geologist and not a historian, the discoveries made by Wolter in recent years and described in *Hooked X* are powerful enough to compel a fundamental rethinking of our view of the American past. The centerpiece of his revelations is that controversial, even contentious artifact known as the Kensington Rune Stone. [See the previous story.—Ed.].

For those who are unfamiliar with it, this is a 200-pound

greywacke sandstone stele found by Swedish immigrant farmer, Olof Ohman, while clearing his land in the largely rural township of Solem, Douglas County, Minnesota, during September 1898. Lying face down and entwined in the roots of a stunted, 30-year-old aspen, the 30-by-16-by-six-inch slab was covered on its face and one side with some sort of runic writing. Ohman brought it to the nearest town, Kensington, where his find was displayed at the local bank.

A badly flawed copy of the inscription was forwarded to the University of Minnesota, where a translation was attempted by Olaus J. Breda. It would take more than another 100 years for scholars, correcting for the imperfect copy, to properly translate the text. The front face reads, "Eight Gotlanders and 22 Norwegians on (this) reclaiming/acquisition journey far west from Vinland. We had a camp by two (shelters?) one day's journey north from this stone. We were fishing one day. After we came home we found 10 men red with blood and death. *Ave Maria.* Save from evil." Inscribed on the side of the stone are the words, "There are 10 men by the sea to look after our ships 14 days journey from this island. Year 1362."

PROFESSIONALS JUMP TO DEBUNK ARTIFACT

Although a professor of Scandinavian languages and literature, Breda's runic knowledge was limited. He hastily proclaimed Ohman's discovery a transparent hoax. Breda was supported by Norway's leading archeologist of the late 19th century, Oluf Rygh, and his colleagues at Northwestern University, in Evanston, Illinois. Their unanimous dismissal of the rune stone was based entirely on its error-ridden facsimile and ruined Ohman's life in an era when a man's word was truly his bond. He never tried to make money off the rune stone; he often cursed the day he found it; and swore he told the whole truth about its discovery unto the hour of his death. With the family reputation ruined, he was shunned and mocked by society to the extent that one of his daughters committed suicide.

While mainstream archeologists and linguists continued to insist that the Kensington Rune Stone was fraudulent, a geologist at the

Minnesota Historical Society, Newton Horace Winchell, undertook a detailed physical analysis of the object for the first time. His tests underscored Ohman's version of events, as particularly confirmed by weathering of the stone, which indicated its inscription was about 500 years old.

"There was strong support for an authentic rune stone date of 1362," Winchell concluded, "and little reason to suspect fraud."

But his 1910 report fell into obscurity beneath the louder denunciations of skeptics, who convinced most of the outside world that the Kensington Rune Stone was a ludicrous forgery. A few amateur researchers had their doubts, however, and wondered if other local evidence might support the rune stone's pre-Columbian authenticity. For examples, they cited the inscribed text for internal evidence. It describes the location of the rune stone as on an "island," even though the object had been found on a farm nowhere near water. Not until 1937, when hydrological surveys were conducted for the state of Minnesota, did investigators learn that the area of discovery was virtually flooded with streams and lakes during the 14th century and for at least 500 years before.

Increasingly dry conditions beginning in the 16th century transfigured the regional landscape into swamps and marsh, until it became the rich pasture Olof Ohman settled in the late 1800s. The hill on which he found the rune stone was indeed an island, although neither he nor anyone else at the time knew it was surrounded by water back in 1362, the inscribed date.

Researchers also pointed out several triangular holes cut into boulders, apparently very long ago, observed along riverways leading toward Ohman's farm; 14th-century Norse seafarers were known to favor triangular mooring holes.

ADDITIONAL FINDS

Not far north and 27 years before the Kensington Rune Stone was discovered, an old fire-steel identical to medieval Norse specimens at Oslo's University Museum emerged from deep beneath the

A SECRET TEMPLAR CODE EMBEDDED WITHIN THE KENSINGTON RUNE STONE?

WHEN THE KENSINGTON RUNE STONE was first discovered, it was quickly labeled a fraud. Critics claimed the founder, Olof Ohman, had carved the rune stone to "prove" Scandinavians had made it to America first, and with perfect timing, just in time for a coming "Christopher Columbus discovered America" celebration by Italian-Americans. More scientific critics later claimed the quirky runic characters were too "modern" and that other characters on the stone were of a form not known in any existing examples. Some had slashes through them; others had odd "punch" marks inside the counters of the letters.

After much research, geologist Scott Wolter and others found characters very much like those on the Kensington Rune Stone in Templar churches in Gotland. This makes sense as the stone said Goths (Gotlanders) were along on the voyage. Further, four characters had slash marks. The "slashed" characters, according to Scott Wolter, seemed to be saying "look at me." When he did, he found that, when deciphered with a "key" called the Easter Dating Table, a secret, "verification date" appeared: 1362—the same date written on the side of the stone in more conventional characters. Important inscriptions were evidently "double dated" in this way by the Templars to ensure that if a stone were found by a rival, and the stone was, for instance, a land claim marker, any nefarious modifications to the stone's original date could be detected with the secret dating method.

bank of the Red River near Climax, Minnesota.

Compelling considerations such as these prompted investigators to seek out professional help of their own in 2000. They contacted the St. Paul-based American Petrographic Services, a firm specializing in the analysis of construction materials to determine suitability, conformance to specifications, or causes of failure. It was and is owned and headed by Scott F. Wolter, a university-trained, certified geologist, who had never even heard of the Kensington Rune Stone. He would conduct its first detailed physical analysis since Winchell's investigation, 90 years before.

With no preconceived notions and indifferent to the outcome of his research, Wolter began using photography with a reflected light microscope, core sampling and examination via a scanning electron microscope. In November, he presented his preliminary findings: the alleged artifact exhibited unmistakable signs of a sub-surface erosional process requiring a minimum of 200 years. In other words, the Kensington Rune Stone was buried for at least a century before Olof Ohman excavated it.

Wolter's conclusion was based on the complete breakdown of mica crystals on the inscribed surface of the stone, compared to his collected samples of slate gravestones from Maine; these showed that biotite mica began to mechanically flake off their surfaces after 197 years, plus or minus five years. Skeptics endeavored to fault his determination by arguing that standards for mica degradation do not exist.

"It is true," he responded to an e-mail inquiry, "that there is no standard for the mica degradation work I performed on the Kensington Rune Stone. The reason is, to my knowledge, I am the first to perform this type of relative-age dating study. Because the biotite mica began to weather off the manmade surfaces of the slate tombstones after approximately 200 years, the Kensington Rune Stone inscription must be older than 200 years (prior to 1898, when it was pulled from the ground), since all the mica had weathered away from the manmade surfaces."

Intrigued, he went on to examine each individual rune through a scanning electron microscope, which revealed some remarkable characteristics. Also noticed was a hitherto-unseen series of dots engraved inside three R-runes. This discovery was highly significant, because such dotted runes occur only on the headstones of 14th-century graves in church cemeteries on the island of Gotland off the coast of Sweden. The Kensington Rune Stone's text dates itself to the same century and mentions eight crewmen from Gotland.

SMOKING GUN

Wolter then studied and replicated the rune stone's first, long-neglected geologic report, released in 1910. Early 21st-century technology confirmed Prof. Winchell's conclusion that the artifact was authentically pre-Columbian. But the proverbial "smoking gun" was the discovery of a single runic letter.

As Wolter explains, "The rare, medieval rune called 'the dotted R' was not known to modern scholars until 1935, yet it is found on the Kensington Rune Stone found in 1898. Interpretation: The presence of the dotted R indicates the Kensington Rune Stone inscription could only have been carved during medieval times."

Unequivocal verification of the Kensington Rune Stone's 14th-century identity was a true scientific triumph, establishing beyond doubt that Scandinavian seafarers arrived in the heartland of North America 130 years before Christopher Columbus left Spain in search of the New World.

But Wolter expanded his research to reveal much more. He discovered that the Kensington Rune Stone was not just some pre-Columbian anomaly proving only that the Norse beat the Spaniards to America. He competently defines it as a land-claim marker. In other words, the men who set it up did so to declare what later became west central Minnesota for themselves. The inscription's date of 1362, Wolter demonstrates, was additionally encoded in the runic text itself, because its Arabic numerals were vulnerable to alteration by interlopers.

After carving, the Kensington Rune Stone was deliberately

THE NEWPORT TOWER RE-EXAMINED IN LIGHT OF WOLTER'S DISCOVERIES

Working from the premise that Prince Henry Sinclair (ca. 1345-ca. 1400) was involved in the construction of the Newport Tower (top photo, facing page), it stands to reason that the architecture of the tower should have similarities to that of northern Scotland, where Prince Henry ruled. Other researchers have offered possible units of measurement used to build the tower: the Scottish ell or the Norwegian alen. Various researchers note that the tower's double flue system in the fireplace is consistent with medieval Scottish architecture. The photos at the botom of the facing page shows an image of ruins of a Cistercian church at Eynhallow in the Orkney Islands (left), side-by-side with a tower archway of the Newport Tower (right). Here is yet another illustration of the possible Scottish origin for the Newport Tower architects. To make the connection to Prince Henry and the Sinclair clan stronger, the abbot in charge of Eynhallow in the mid-12th-century was Abbot Lawrence, previously known as Henry Sinclair of Rye. Further, prominent solar and lunar alignments have been found to be visible through the windows of the tower from viewing stations inside.

buried, and triangular-shaped holes were drilled into glacial boulders not far away; these were used to triangulate and relocate the precise position of the buried rune stone. The directional marker holes are no speculation, but were recently found, and do indeed still indicate the original location of the Kensington Rune Stone's discovery by Olof Ohman.

Wolter goes still further in his quest for information about the artifact to discover the identity of the man who carved its inscription: a Cistercian monk from Gotland, the same Swedish island cited in the runic text. The Cistercians were monastic, Gnostic Christians, founders of the Knights Templar, who survived the latter's immolation during the early 14th century by migrating from France to other parts of Europe, including Gotland. Templars were still residents of the island at the time the Kensington Rune Stone was carved in 1362. According to Wolter, its inscription "includes information related to who the party was, where their location was, when they were there and why."

The key unlocking this information is the mysterious "hooked X," which not only appears on the Kensington Rune Stone, but among several other runic texts in Europe and pre-Columbian North America. As Wolter explains, "the hooked X symbol is an important coded runic symbol likely created by Cistercian monks. The 'X' is symbolic of the allegorical representation of the duality and balance of man and woman, and heaven and earth. The 'hook' in the X is symbolic of the child or offspring, representative of the continuation and perpetuation of the 'Goddess' ideology through common bloodlines and thought."

His interpretation is substantiated by medieval scholars long aware of the proto-Tempar Cistercians' unusual theology.

Appropriately, "the hooked X appears on dated inscriptions from two exploration parties during a 40-year period," inclusive of the Kensington Rune Stone text's creation. This peculiar glyph is especially helpful in authenticating a runic inscription, because it is highly unlikely to have been known to a hoaxer, appears on few artifacts, and has been competently dated to the late Middle Ages, thereby helping to establish not only the authenticity, but the time parameters of a particular object.

Accordingly, Wolter gives us the Kensington Rune Stone in the context of other, related finds. Among the best known is Rhode Island's Newport Tower. Ordained by mainstream archeologists as nothing more than the ruin of an 17th-century mill supposedly owned by the family of none other than Benedict Arnold, Wolter instead demonstrates that the stone structure in Touro Park "was built using architecture that is not consistent with pre-Colonial construction practices before the first known recording in Benedict Arnold's will in 1677 [this was an ancestor of the more famous Benedict Arnold]. . . . Since the standard unit of measurement used in construction throughout New England in the 17th century was the English foot, the Newport Tower [which was laid out in the Norwegian short *alen*] was not built by 17th-century Colonists."

MYSTERIOUS TOWER EXPLAINED

He cites dating procedures applied in 1997 to the structure by Danish professor Andre J. Bethune, whose carbon-14 analysis indicated that, in Bethune's words, "the Newport Tower was standing in the years 1440 to 1480." Wolter shows that its close resemblance to sacred buildings in medieval Europe and the Near East—such as Scotland's mid-12th-century Eynhallow Church in Orkney or Jerusalem's Templum Domini—defines the Newport Tower as a baptistery additionally employed for navigational purposes.

Wolter quotes a prominent researcher, the late James Whittall, who pointed out that "the tool marks created in the dressing out of the stonework (on the Newport Tower) can directly be related to tools before 1400. These marks are unique and unknown when compared to tool marks noted in Colonial stonework. . . . The single and double-splay windows have prototypes in medieval Europe and in the northern isles of Scotland in the 1300s in churches and the bishop's palace in Orkney. . . . The walls were covered with a plaster stucco finish, both interior and exterior. Stucco finishing started in

THE 'HOOKED X,'
THE NARRAGANSETT STONE
AND THE SPIRIT POND
RUNE STONES

THERE ARE OTHER AMERICAN stones with scripts and quirky characters quite similar to the Kensington Rune Stone (including "hooked X's" (left), punch marks and slashes), all of which rarely if ever appeared in old futhark-based Viking scripts. Obviously, these stones are not of Viking origin. Now, in light of the discoveries of geologist Scott Wolter, scholars are taking a second look at several other controversial ancient American artifacts including the

Spirit Pond (Maine) rune stones (one of the three known Spirit Pond stones shown at top on the facing page), the 300-lb. Westford (Massachusetts) Boat Stone (shown right) and the Narragansett (Rhode Island) Stone  (bottom). Found in Rhode Island's Narragansett Bay, this runic inscription is only visible for 20 minutes a day, at low tide. (Carbon-dating of the floorboards of a nearby long house yielded a date of 1405.) A hooked X is clearly visible on nearly every line of the Spirit Pond stone shown. At bottom is a photo of the Narragansett Stone with a hooked X. On the facing page is shown one of many hooked X's from the Kensington Rune Stone. As far as the Westford Boat Stone, weathering patterns of the carving seem consistent with that of a 600-year-old artifact, and the carving resembles a 14th-century knarr. Incidentally, experts now say secret dates were embedded on the Spirit Pond Rune Stones, verifying Easter Table dates of 1401 (once) and 1402 (three times).

the 1200s and is a feature known in Orkney and Shetland. . . . There is no archeological parallel in Colonial New England for the Newport Tower and its specific architectural features."

These and numerous other supporting details leave no doubt about the tower's pre-Columbian provenance.

Wolter goes to describe several other pieces of evidence for the medieval European impact on this continent, and for the presentation alone of these otherwise little-known artifacts, his book is especially valuable. To him, they are all fragments of an interrelating mosaic, the final image of which tends to reveal a post-Templar interest in North America.

Traces of this shadowy presence are scattered throughout a diverse collection of stone inscriptions and archeological sites from Minnesota's Kensington Rune Stone to similar texts and engraved illustrations in New England.

THE NARRAGANSETT STONE

Among the least known, yet most convincing discoveries of its kind, is a one-line lithic inscription found near Pojac Point in Narragansett Bay, an estuary on the north side of Rhode Island Sound. The mostly submerged, two-ton glacial boulder's difficult accessibility some 60 feet from shore in often rough water says much for the pre-Columbian credibility of the runes etched into its top, which just protrudes above the surface of the sea and is continuously washed by wave action. These conditions argue strongly against the probability of a hoax.

Wolter found that each of the nine glyphs was approximately two inches long and cut one-half inch deep. The first rune he was able to identify was a version of H dated to the late Middle Ages. This suspected period was confirmed when he located a telltale "hooked X" on the Narragansett Stone. Its location in New England's largest estuary, which functions as an expansive natural harbor, tends to support the probability of visiting seafarers who used this location as a perfect headquarters from which to navigate the interior. The Sakonnet River, Mount Hope Bay and the southern tidal part of the Taunton River are all part of Narragansett Bay.

Other "hooked X" specimens were uncovered far from the Narragansett Stone in 1971. They were found shallowly buried along the shores of Spirit Pond, not far from the Maine coast, near Popham Beach.

Like other accidental discoveries unfortunate enough to have been made by unaccredited persons, the three Spirit Pond stones were automatically deemed fraudulent by mainstream opinion, and tossed into the Maine State Museum at Hallowell, where Wolter took some 1,700 photographs of them from 2006 to 2007. His examination showed that one of the stones, apparently illustrated with a map, was strangely oriented with east at the top and north to the left, something a forger would have been unlikely to do. Yet, until 1500, medieval maps were identically oriented to place Jerusalem, in the east, at the top.

His colleague, amateur linguist Richard Nielsen, had already determined an internal date of "1401" from the Maine artifacts' runic texts. Only later, just 300 yards from Spirit Pond, did archeologists uncover the remains of a Norse-style sod building, and radiocarbon-dated its floorboards to circa A.D. 1405.

Wolter was likewise impressed by the convincing antiquity of a very large granite boulder illustrated with the outlines of surrounding topography, and located in a town near the Merrimac River, as it flows through the northwest section of Middlesex County, Massachusetts. Known as the Tyngsboro Map Stone, it is an amazingly accurate representation of the local Merrimac River-Lake Winnipesaukee watershed.

"I was struck by the advanced stage of weathering of the man-made lines," Wolter recalls. "I peeled back some of the lichen, and there was virtually no difference between the cut lines and the glacial surfaces. The weathering actually surprised me. Whoever carved this did it long ago."

THE WESTFORD KNIGHT

Not far from the Tyngsboro Map Stone, in the same county, a better-known Massachusetts site he investigated is the Westford Knight allegedly illustrated on glacially striated, mica-schist bedrock. The image had been familiar to generations of Westford residents, but was only professionally photographed for the first time immediately following World War II. The findings were published shortly thereafter in *The Ruins of Greater Ireland and New England* by W.B. Goodwin (Meador Press, Boston, 1946). To protect the site, Goodwin never revealed its precise whereabouts. Some years after his death, however, a determined reader, Frank Glynn, eventually found the image, which had been created by punch-holes made with a hammer. The unorthodox illustration supposedly portrayed a helmeted knight-at-arms, complete with sword and shield.

By the time Wolter examined it in 2006, he was unable to make out anything resembling a human figure, perhaps because it eroded away in the decades of exposure to the elements after moss covering the illustration was removed. In any case, he did clearly discern the pecked outline of a broadsword, which according to Fitchburg, Massachusetts historian Michael Kaulback "was identified by British antiquarians as a large 'hand-and-a-half wheel pommel blade' of the 13th or 14th century" (*Discovering the Mysteries of Ancient America*, New Page Books, NJ 2006). This would make the image approximately contemporaneous with Minnesota's Kensington Rune Stone.

A short walking distance from the Westford Knight, the J.V. Fletcher Library displays a 300-pound glacial granite boulder depicting a sailing vessel in the company of an arrow and three glyphs.

"All had been made using a pecking technique similar to the Westford sword," Wolter writes. "The stone had been found only a couple of miles from the library in 1932 by a landowner named William Wyman. He moved the 'boat stone' into a shed and kept it in his possession until one of his descendants gave it to the library in the early 1960s. The fact that the pecking technique was similar to the Westford Knight didn't mean the carver was the same person,

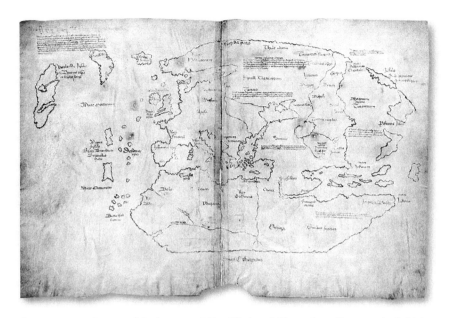

Controversy has swirled around the Vinland Map since it came to light in the 1950s, many scholars suspecting it was a hoax meant to prove that Vikings were the first Europeans to land in North America—a claim confirmed by a 1960 archeological find. Doubts about the map linger even after the use of carbon dating as a way of establishing the age of an object. "All the tests that we have done over the past five years—on the materials and other aspects— do not show any signs of forgery," Rene Larsen, rector of the School of Conservation under the Royal Danish Academy of Fine Arts, said in an interview. U.S. researchers have carbon dated the map to about 1440. Scholars believe it was produced for a church council at Basel, Switzerland, the same year. The Vinland Map is not a "Viking map," but, if it is genuine, it shows that the New World was known not only to Norsemen but also to other Europeans at the very least half a century before Columbus's voyage.

but it could be an indication of the particular period when they were made. I was certain the weathering of both the Westford Boat Stone and the Westford Knight were not made in the past several decades, and could very well be many hundreds of years old."

These artifacts have become invaluable for the validation of their pre-Columbian authenticity, thanks to an accredited scientist, a professional geologist. As such, he has removed them from the uncertain speculation of amateur theorists. More importantly, Scott Wolter shows that they are pieces of a puzzle far greater than its individual parts. The bigger picture emerging with breathtaking credibility from his research reveals the surprising extent and depth of Norse impact on our continent long before Christopher Columbus was born.

VINLAND MAP AUTHENTIC

Significantly, as the first copies of *The Hooked X* were rolling off the press, every word the author wrote was being powerfully underscored by Rene Larsen, rector of the School of Conservation at the Royal Danish Academy of Fine Arts. Last July, he and his colleagues—all world-class authorities in their respective fields—announced during Copenhagen's International Conference on the History of Cartography that the so-called Vinland Map was authentic. Their five-year investigation established that this document, long contested by conventional scholars, was a compilation of Norse voyages to and exploration of North America beginning after A.D. 1000.

The map's portrayed landmass, identified as *Vinilanda Insula*, encompasses an area from Maine in the north to the Carolinas in the south; from the Atlantic seaboard to the Susquehanna River in central Pennsylvania. The Danes' contemporary announcement was a timely vindication of Wolter's conclusions.

The first line in his book, opening a foreword by Niven Sinclair, proclaims, "History needs to be rewritten." And so it has been, in *The Hooked X.*   ◆

BIBLIOGRAPHY:
    Wolter, Scott F., *The Hooked X, Key to the Secret History of North America*, North Star Press of St. Cloud, Inc., MN, 2009.

Frank Joseph is a supporter of what has been called the diffusionist approach to prehistory. He was born in Chicago in 1944. Joseph is the author of the books Atlantis and Other Lost Worlds *and* The Lost Civilization of Lemuria. *He was an assistant editor at* The Ancient American, *a quarterly magazine investigating possible visits to the Americas from the Old World before Columbus.*

Oak Island Pit Still Confounds

Oak Island is a 140-acre island off Nova Scotia. The tree-covered island is located in Mahone Bay. Oak Island is the location of the so-called Money Pit, a site of numerous excavations to recover treasure believed by some to be buried there. Is the Oak Island pit a Templar structure? A pirate's creation? Were oak timbers actually found as often as reported? And the disappearance of the inscription stone that was allegedly found in the pit has further muddied the issue. Several documented treasure recovery attempts ended in collapsed excavations and flooding—even death. This illustration depicts salvage attempts and what several early excavators allege to have found.

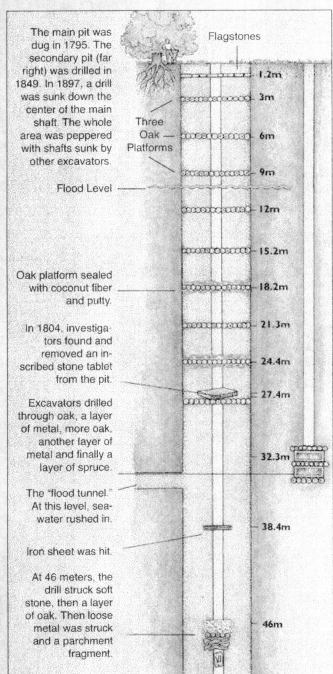

The main pit was dug in 1795. The secondary pit (far right) was drilled in 1849. In 1897, a drill was sunk down the center of the main shaft. The whole area was peppered with shafts sunk by other excavators.

Flagstones

Three Oak Platforms

Flood Level

1.2m

3m

6m

9m

12m

15.2m

Oak platform sealed with coconut fiber and putty.

18.2m

21.3m

In 1804, investigators found and removed an inscribed stone tablet from the pit.

24.4m

27.4m

Excavators drilled through oak, a layer of metal, more oak, another layer of metal and finally a layer of spruce.

32.3m

The "flood tunnel." At this level, seawater rushed in.

Iron sheet was hit.

38.4m

At 46 meters, the drill struck soft stone, then a layer of oak. Then loose metal was struck and a parchment fragment.

46m

ANCIENT VISITORS
To The Americas:
THE EVIDENCE

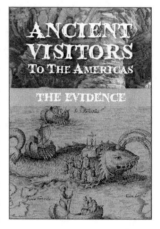

Ancient Visitors to the Americas: The Evidence covers the mountain of evidence that exists—consistently suppressed my mainstream historians—proving that not only Vikings and other European cultures made it to America centuries before Columbus, but that Asians and Arabs made it to North and South America as well. This book will serve as a whirlwind tour of the subject and is by no means an encompassing study. If it were, the book could literally have been thousands of pages long! Articles included in this fascinating anthology include ones on the Kensington Rune Stone, the Templars and Vikings in America, the Irish in ancient America, ancient copper miners in North America from the bronze age era, the fractious Burrows Cave debate, the ancient white ancestors of many American Indian tribes, Phoenicians in America, ancient Chinese and Japanese artifacts found in Central and South America, the Newport Tower mystery, pre-Columbian maps of the Americas and the many Old World scripts found carved in stones in the Americas—including one of Minoan origin—plus much, much more. Softcover, 183 pages, $25 plus $4 S&H inside the U.S. from AFP, P.O. Box 15877, Washington, D.C. 20003. Call 1-888-699-6397 toll free to charge or visit our online store at www.americanfreepress.net to order.

AMERICAN FREE PRESS ORDERING COUPON

Item#	Description/Title	Qty	Cost Ea.	Total
			SUBTOTAL	
		Add S&H on books*		
	Send me a 1-year USA subscription to AFP for $49			
	Send me a 2-year USA subscription to AFP for $89			
			TOTAL	

*S&H ON BOOKS: Add $4 S&H on orders up to $25. Add $6 S&H on orders from $25.01 to $50. Add $8 S&H on orders from $50.01 to $75. Add $1o flat S&H on orders over $100. Note: Outside the U.S. email shop@AmericanFreePress.net for S&H. You may also subscribe to AFP or buy books at www.AmericanFreePress.net

PAYMENT OPTIONS: ❏ CHECK/MO ❏ VISA ❏ MC ❏ DISCOVER ❏ AMEX

Card # _____

Expiration Date _____ Signature _____

VAA114

CUSTOMER INFORMATION:

NAME _____

ADDRESS _____

CITY/STATE/ZIP _____

RETURN WITH PAYMENT TO: AMERICAN FREE PRESS, P.O. Box 15877, Washington, D.C. 20003. Call 1-888-699-63977 toll free to charge to major credit cards.

CPSIA information can be obtained
at www.ICGtesting.com
Printed in the USA
FFOW02n1639160315
11773FF